T0266466

A Muslim's Reflections
on
Democratic Capitalism

Muhammad Abdul-Rauf

American Enterprise Institute for Public Policy Research
Washington and London

Distributed to the Trade by National Book Network, 15200 NBN Way, Blue Ridge Summit, PA 17214. To order call toll free 1-800-462-6420 or 1-717-794-3800. For all other inquiries please contact the AEI Press, 1150 Seventeenth Street, N.W., Washington, D.C. 20036 or call 1-800-862-5801.

Library of Congress Cataloging in Publication Data

Abdul-Rauf, Muhammad, 1917–
  A Muslim's reflections on democratic capitalism.

  (AEI studies ; 393)
  Bibliography: p.
  1. Economics—Religious aspects—Islam.   I. Title.
II. Series.
BP173.75.A182   1984   297'.19785   83-15530
ISBN 0-8447-3537-X

AEI Studies 393

ISBN 978-0-8447-3537-5

Contents

President's Foreword

For nine years Dr. Muhammad Abdul-Rauf was the esteemed director of the Islamic Center in Washington, D.C. In 1978, he contributed a seminal essay, "The Islamic Doctrine of Economics and Contemporary Thought," to the first volume of essays from the American Enterprise Institute's summer institutes on Religion and Economics, *Capitalism and Socialism: A Theological Inquiry*. In the present book Dr. Rauf uses the ideals of democratic capitalism, as they developed in Jewish-Christian writings, to describe the alternative vision of Islam, proceeding throughout by comparison and contrast.

The detailed unfolding of Dr. Rauf's book is fascinating. He has carefully searched the holy Qur'ān and *Al-Hadīth*, the sayings and recorded deeds of the Prophet Muhammad, finding most features of a democratic capitalist economy to be in accord with Islamic revelation. Like democratic capitalism, Islam favors free enterprise and private ownership. The Prophet encouraged increased production, trade, and commerce, indicating at the same time that he favored only a limited role for the state in the regulation of trade. In addition, Islam teaches individual liberty, the right to own property, equality of opportunity (but not of wealth), equality among individuals, and the important responsibility of every Muslim male to support his family, including adult children and distant relatives.

Rauf emphasizes the enormous effect that this responsibility has in stimulating economic activity in Islamic society. In Islam, the accumulation of wealth is a just aspiration, but carries with it many obligations, particularly to the generous giving of alms. In Islam, accumulated wealth is to be redistributed through alms, charity, and the division of a Muslim's estate following his death.

With the publication of *A Muslim's Reflections On Democratic Capitalism*, the American Enterprise Institute is extending its studies of the connection between religious values and systems of political economy, conducted by AEI's Center for Religion, Philosophy, and Public Policy. Since 1980, the Center has pioneered in examining the religious dimensions of political economy.

WILLIAM J. BAROODY
President
American Enterprise Institute

Foreword

This work is an important Muslim response to an important book. Dr. Rauf first sets out in scholarly fashion and in a tone that reflects the author's profound devotion to Islam the principles of what is now coming to be known as Islamic economics, revealing the profoundly moral character of all economic activity from the Islamic point of view. He then turns to an analysis of Michael Novak's *Spirit of Democratic Capitalism*, complaining quite rightly about the exclusion of Islam whenever the Judeo-Christian tradition is considered in the West. He also points to the different position of Islam concerning such questions as race and the importance of the moral order, which must always prevail. For the most part, however, Dr. Rauf agrees with Novak's major theses, including his criticism of Marxism and socialism. He defends with courage the traditional Islamic view of the legitimacy of being wealthy provided that the wealth is gained by legitimate means and that the religious tax is paid. On this important point he separates himself from so many contemporary Muslim writers who present the Socialist point of view thinly disguised as Islamic teaching. While concurring with Novak in his criticism of Juergen Moltmann and Liberation Theology, Dr. Rauf nevertheless takes issue with the thesis that specifically Christian doctrines such as the Trinity were responsible for the rise of democratic capitalism.

Finally, Dr. Rauf turns to an Islamic response to Novak. Despite the clamor of those who employ the epithet of socialism in the Islamic world, he shows that Islam agrees with democratic capitalism, as depicted by Novak, on many basic points, such as emphasizing private initiative, open and free markets, and free enterprise, while insisting upon the divine and moral character of economic activity. Among the most noteworthy pages of this book are the author's criticism of so-called Islamic socialism. He points to the vast chasm that separates the Islamic idea of equal opportunity from the Socialist goal of equality of fortune. While Islam also contrasts with capitalism in that the Qur'ān emphasizes the "double ownership" of property by both man and God, Dr. Rauf is careful to point out the similarities and areas of cooperation which can exist between Islamic teachings and the "theology of economics" of democratic capitalism developed by Novak. Dr. Rauf, therefore, goes far beyond many modern Muslim writers who simply repeat that Islam is neither socialism nor capitalism but neither provide an in-depth criticism of socialism with an Arab or Islamic veneer nor seek to understand the value system of the democratic capitalist system. At this present juncture of Islamic history when so many alien ideologies parading as Islam are eclipsing the veritable teachings of the Islamic religion and bringing about great calamities upon many parts of the Islamic world, the work of Dr. Rauf stands as an important statement. It should turn the eyes and minds of both Muslims and students of Islam to the analysis of the theses of Novak's major opus and to a reexamination of Islamic teachings as they concern the claims, ideals, and practices of both socialism and democratic capitalism.

PROFESSOR SEYYED HOSSEIN NASR
Temple University

Preface

Trained as a student of Islamic theology and Qur'ānic exegesis, I have never been an economist. My theological and educational training has been well invested in various posts held since my graduation from the ancient University of Al-Azhar, Cairo, in the early 1940s. Besides teaching at Al-Azhar and teaching and planning at the Islamic Institute of Kuwait in the latter part of the 1940s, I held a professorial position at the University of Malaya for nearly nine years, beginning early in 1955. From April 1971 to December 1980 I was the director of the Islamic Center in Washington, D.C., having held a similar position at the Islamic Cultural Center of New York the preceding five years.

My jobs at the Islamic centers in America entailed tremendous administrative, counseling, and teaching responsibilities, as well as religious and social duties. Fifteen years of continuous study at Al-Azhar, the world renowned center for the study of Islamic culture and tradition, and five years of study at London and Cambridge Universities in the early 1950s helped prepare me to shoulder the responsibilities assigned to me in Egypt, Kuwait, Malaysia, and the United States.

In the course of my work at the Islamic Cultural Center of New York and the Islamic Center in Washington, D.C., I was often invited to deliver speeches and lectures across the United States and Canada on a wide range of subjects. Despite the variety of themes, I found that they could be handled on the basis of my theological training even when the topic touched, as it often did, on the political crisis of the Middle East.

In 1978, however, my dear friend, William Baroody, Sr., president of the American Enterprise Institute for Public Policy Research in Washington, D.C., asked me to participate in a summer program on capitalism and socialism to be sponsored by AEI and the University of Syracuse. He suggested that I contribute two papers, remarking on the growing interest in the relationship between people's beliefs and their economic values and practices. "We should like to explore this relationship," he said. Under the gentle but insistent pressure of my distinguished friend, I yielded after some hesitation.

To prepare myself for this difficult assignment, I had to read some economic literature in both Arabic and English, especially that relevant to Islamic economics. I admired the pioneering work of Maulana al-Mawdudi[1] and the works of Abdallah al-Arabi, Ahmad al-Najjār, and Isa Abduh.[2] Yet I could not gain sufficient insight to help me address such a highly specialized non-Muslim audience on a topic outside the scope of my life's experience. I then turned to the original sources of Islam: to the Holy Qur'ān, which I had early learned by heart in preparation for admission to the primary stage of al-Azhar. I also turned to Al-Hadīth, the sayings and recorded deeds of the Prophet Muhammad, which stands as a supplement to and a commentary on the Holy Qur'ān.

Reflecting carefully on Qur'ānic words and Al-Hadīth texts relevant to the subject, I came to the conclusion that they, as spiritual revelations focusing on moral guidance, could not be expected to provide a "scientific theory" of economics, or, for that matter, a theory of any other scientific pursuit that must be based on empirical research. Through sustained effort and deep reflection and concentration on the relevant Qur'ānic passages, I was able to discover a Qur'ānic framework of economic moral guidance that I prefer to call the Islamic doctrine of economics. The result of my contribution to the seminar was a lengthy essay published under the title *The Islamic Doctrine of Economics and Contemporary Economic Thought*.[3]

Ever since then, my relationship with AEI has been fairly close. I have attended the institute's seminars, especially those at which theological themes were discussed and in which Christian clergymen and Jewish scholars participated. I was impressed by the erudition and insight of some of the participants, particularly Dr. Michael Novak, who often conducted these seminars.

An often-recurring theme in those useful seminars was the concept of democratic capitalism. We are all familiar with the battle waged between capitalism and socialism. In spite of the appeal of its rhetoric, socialism has faded away. Its utopian dreams have proved to be an illusion, though socialism is still clung to in one form or another by some East European and third-world governments. Capitalism, too, has modified itself and has welcomed some socialistic reforms within its system. It is no longer simple capitalism but *democratic* capitalism. It has also felt a need for a philosophy as a moral-intellectual basis. Dr. Novak, a renowned theologian and eminent writer, has taken up this task, seeking to trace a theological foundation for democratic capitalism from the moral-cultural values rooted in Judeo-Christian traditions. This theme has been reiterated again and again by Dr. Novak, and it permeates much of his recent writing. It has also been a subject of interest to many of the scholars associated with the American Enterprise Institute. The major work on democratic capitalism, however, is a book written by Dr. Novak, entitled *The Spirit of Democratic Capitalism.*[4]

I was fortunate to have access to the manuscript of this work, and I have thoroughly enjoyed reading it. Struck by some of the views enunciated by the author, I was often intrigued by the comparison between Dr. Novak's ideas and those instilled in me by my own faith and traditions. As a Muslim from the third world, I wondered whether an assessment of the author's views and analysis would be of interest not only to experts in Muslim homelands but also to readers in the West. I therefore wanted to write down my reflections and responses as a student of Islam to the views and theories presented in this work, which presumes to be launching a new discipline, the theology of economics. I hope this small volume will be a modest contribution to this new field.

In chapter 1, I endeavor to formulate the concept of Islamic economics as it can be derived from the previously mentioned sources. This will help serve as a background for my arguments and comments in the following chapter, in which Dr. Novak's views are analyzed and examined. The last chapter summarizes my views and impressions as a Muslim.

Notes

1. Al-Mawdudi was a leading Pakistani reformer and great Muslim author. His relevant writings include *Between Islam and Contemporary Systems,* written in 1937, and *Problems of Economics and Their Solution by Islam,* written in prison late in the 1940s. Both were combined and published in Damascus in 1960.

2. These Egyptian authors sought to formulate an Islamic economic theory. Al-Najjar, in particular, is known for his pioneering work in setting up and developing Islamic banks and is currently the secretary general of the Federation of the Islamic Banks.

3. American Enterprise Institute, 1979.

4. Michael Novak, *The Spirit of Democratic Capitalism* (New York: An American Enterprise Institute/Simon & Schuster Publication, 1982).

1

Characteristics of the Concept of
Islamic Economics

Of all the creatures on earth, man is the only one who carries the burden of responsibility: responsibility for his own welfare, responsibility for the well-being of his environment, and responsibility before his Lord, the Creator of all things. Man moves around, not just mechanically or blindly or instinctively, but consciously, deliberately, and voluntarily. Although he is a child of nature and depends on her bounties, which are provided by his Lord, man can be her master. With his intelligence and his nimble hands, man can harness nature to serve him and to improve the quality of his life. With his creative power and with a memory that stores acquired knowledge, he can build on his experiences and shape his future.

Like other living creatures, man is created with certain basic needs that have to be satisfied in order for him to survive. Yet, unlike the needs of other living things, man's needs are difficult to satisfy: the means of satisfying human needs are not readily available or easily accessible or immediately consumable. They have to be picked, hunted, fished, dug out, or grown and harvested; and they often must be treated and prepared for human consumption. In the process, man has learned many vocations. With the increasing world population and the scarcity of raw materials, man has learned to organize the distribution of the available resources. He became a trader and calculating businessman. In his drive to improve his living conditions, man made life more complex and created other needs. There was improvement in every aspect of human earthly life, followed by immense discoveries and countless inventions.

Man's struggle for physical survival on earth is described as materialistic or economic, but man is not merely an economic animal. Being so intelligent and reflective, man grasped the notion that it would be senseless if this earthly life was in itself his ultimate end. It is full of conflict, pain, misery, and suffering; and it comes to a sad end! If the end of man were the same as that of the animal, what

1

difference would it make to be a human being? What is the value of the human brain? Is it merely to be invested in vanishing pleasures mixed with pain? Would the end of a peaceful charitable soul be like that of a despotic ruler who sent thousands or millions of innocent human victims to suffocate in gas chambers?

Man's Creator came to his aid. Through divine revelation and the Prophetic missions and the Scriptures—starting with the mission of Adam and ending with that of Muhammad (A.D. 610–632)—man has learned that the earthly life is not purposeless. It is a transitory, short existence, a preparatory ground for a more meaningful and lasting life when all human beings will be raised and brought to account before God to be punished or rewarded according to their earthly records. Through these divine missions, man has also learned that he is more than an economic animal. He is a spiritual being as well, a combination of a soul and a body. His salvation lies in his ability to strike a balance between his material and his spiritual needs, to serve the purpose of his creation. In the Holy Qur'ān, believed by Muslims to be God's word revealed to the Prophet Muhammad, God states: "I created the jinn and human kind only that they might worship Me [51:56]." In a tradition, God is quoted to have said: "I was a hidden treasure. I wanted to be known. I created the world, and through Me they know Me."[1] Another Qur'ānic verse reads: "The seven heavens and the earth and all that is therein praise Him [God], and there is not a thing but hymns His praise but you understand not their praise [17:44]."

The birds, the beasts, the grass, the flowers, the trees, the stars, the wind, the sand, the stone, the cells, the atom, the electron—if all hymn and glorify the name of their Creator, God (Whose existence alone is real, perfect, inherent, eternal), and if they, in their hymn, in their dynamism, and in their silence, all stand as unspoken evidence of the omnipresence, omniscience, and omnipotence of their Lord, then mankind has a full share in this silent praise of the Almighty. Yet man also serves his Lord consciously, deliberately, and purposefully. This is man's special privilege. The Creator has endowed mankind with intellect, with the power to distinguish between good and evil, right and wrong, what is useful and what is harmful, and what is worthy and what is unworthy. Man is also endowed by his Creator with a sense of dignity and is to be treated accordingly, alive or dead. Man is thus favored by the Almighty as the cream of all His creations. As the Holy Qur'ān says: "Verily We have honored the children of Adam [17:70]."

To help man fulfill his needs, God not only provided countless and endless bounties in earth and in heaven, but also created man with inner motives that impel him to work and struggle to secure the means of satisfying his needs with eagerness and pleasure, whether those needs are physical, psychological, social, recreational, or spiritual. Without this motivation, human life would be not only dull and boring but also burdensome, disagreeable, and intolerable. In fact, the total earthly life of man consists of his struggle to respond to these inner urges, and his success depends on his compliance with the patterns of behavior within the divine guidance of the Almighty God. These inner urges include the economic motive—call it, if you wish, acquisitiveness, materialism, craving for material security, or simply love of wealth. It is the emotional factor that prompts the human individual to work hard in order to survive in a satisfactory manner. Among all motivating factors, the economic urge seems to be the most significant and certainly the most pervasive. It is with us from the cradle to the grave without interruption. Its satisfaction is essential for the fulfillment of other needs. A person with an empty stomach loses his appetite for other pleasures.

It would be naive and unfair to condemn summarily these human inner motives, particularly the factor of economic stimulus. They are created for legitimate ends. Even the sexual urge, which may seem to have sensual gratification as its end, has its biological, psychological, cultural, and demographic objectives. In their primitive state, however, these motives are crude and therefore need refining and polishing. They have been so created to test man's ability to modify and control them, to resist their excessive demands and to see how man can subjugate them to his intellectual reasoning and his moral conscience as nourished by the divine teachings. Hence, abstention, self-control, resistance to evil desires, and moderation are among the virtues strongly emphasized in Islam. In view of the importance of these motives, the individual's intention is taken into account. Therefore, evil intentions are condemned, and believers are warned against obeying evil desires. An unfulfilled good intention is rewarded onefold, but a fulfilled good intention is promised a manifold reward. As the Holy Qur'ān says:

And follow not desire that it beguiles you from the way of God [38:26].

But as for him who feared to stand before his Lord and restrained his soul from lust, indeed Paradise will be his abode [79:40–41].

And [by] the soul and Him who perfected it, and inspired it [with the distinction between] what is wrong for it and what is right for it. He is indeed successful who causes it to be pure, and he is indeed a failure who stunts it [91:7–10].

3

Verily the [human] soul enjoins evil, save that whereon my Lord has mercy [12:53].

And say unto them—Act! God will behold your actions, and so will the Prophet and the believers, and you will be brought back to the One who knows the invisible and the visible realities, and He will tell you [the result] of what you used to do [9:105].

So, whosoever does good an atom's weight will see it [99:7].

And God is aware of what you do [63:11].

Indeed I shall not cause the work of any working person of you, male or female, to be lost [3:195].

Whosoever brings a good deed will receive tenfold the like thereof, while whosoever brings an ill deed will be recompensed according to his evil; and no injustice shall be done unto any of them [6:160].

The Prophet Muhammad said:

The value of an action depends on the accompanying intention. And everyone will only receive [the reward for] what he intended to do.[2]

Whosoever intended to do a good deed but could not do it, it will be counted for him as one full good deed. And whosoever intended to do a good deed and actually did it, it will be counted for him tenfold.[3]

A person is responsible only for his own deeds, however, not for those of others, no matter how close they are to him, whether a parent or a child, an ancestor or an offspring. The notion of an original sin is alien to Muslim thinking, as are the ideas of an inherited sense or feeling of guilt, redemption, and human bondage. According to the Prophet, "Every child is born innocent and pure."[4] The Holy Qur'ān says:

Every soul is a pledge for its own deeds [74:38].

And that man has only that for which he makes efforts [53:39].

No burdened soul can bear another's burden, and if one heavily burdened [soul] should cry for [help with] its load, naught of it will be lifted even though he [unto whom he cries] be a kin of him [35:18].

The Prophet also said: When the child of Adam dies, the register of his deeds closes, except for three things: a continued charity [like endowments], contribution to human knowledge [like a good book], and the prayers of a righteous child.[5]

Islam thus recognizes the inner motives of the individual and their value when they are controlled by the moral conscience, nourished, as was mentioned earlier, by divine guidance. They provide fuel, so to speak, for man's journey through the earthly life, and the religious teachings guide man in that journey safely and correctly. Man's earthly journey, however, has to be one of hard work and struggle, of toil and sweat, pain and pleasure, want and sufficiency, failure and success—but always with a trust in God and in anticipation of happiness on the day when man will meet with his Lord. Just imagine a world where life was easy, with the means of filling all man's needs immediately accessible and readily consumable while man is what he is. He would not have to sweat, hunt, or plant and harvest. There would be no need for him to trade, speculate, or invent or to bake and cook—how dull life would be! There would be no progress, but only laziness, stupidity, obesity, and corruption. As the Holy Qur'ān says: "And if Allah were to enlarge the provisions for His servants, they would surely rebel in the earth, but He sends down by measure as He wills . . . [42:27]."

A believer toils, but he knows that he struggles not only to earn his living but also to win God's pleasure. The Prophet shook hands with a youth and asked him why his hand was so rough. When the youth answered that it was rough because he used an ax to till the land, the Prophet said: "This is a hand beloved to God and His Messenger."[6] In another version of the encounter, he kissed the hand and said, "It is a hand that shall never burn in fire!"[7] The Holy Qur'ān implies that to struggle for a living is tantamount to fighting to protect the faith,[8] a fact stressed by the Prophet when he spoke of a man with a strong physique who passed through the place where the Prophet was organizing his men to repel an attack. When someone remarked that he wished that the youth would enlist in the defense of the faith, the Prophet retorted: "If he was going to work for his own living or the needs of his dependents or to help his neighbor he was also struggling in the way of God!"[9] The Qur'ān proclaims: "He [God] has made the earth subservient to you. So travel in its [various] paths and eat of His Providence [67:15]."

For man to achieve his earthly mission, as has been hinted at previously, he must pursue a straight path in which the demands of his spiritual and material natures are balanced and coordinated. There is no sharp line dividing the two. An action may be spiritual and worldly at one and the same time. Payment of the zakat (alms for the poor) and making a pilgrimage to Mecca at least once in a lifetime—two of the Five Ritual Pillars of Islam—are spiritual duties involving material costs. Yet an action that seems purely materialistic such as trading or working in a factory or at one's desk, is given a spiritual flavor. In the midst of his worldly occupation, a Muslim has God in his heart and on his tongue and is aware of His watchful eye, a guarantee against dishonesty and fraud. Moreover, Islam teaches practices of a ritual nature that lead to a remembrance of God. Such practices and remembrances meet the needs of the soul in its yearning for spiritual elevation.

The balance between spiritual and physical needs ensures the integrity of human life in an orderly, agreeable way. Tilting either way upsets this delicate balance. Islam opposes denying the body what it demands, but does not condone greed or excesses. A believer must seek a middle road, a line of moderation. As the Holy Qur'ān says:

> And thus we have made you a nation of the middle way [2:143].
>
> And let not your hand be chained to your neck, nor should you open it too widely [17:29].
>
> O children of Adam! Wear your adornment at every place of worship; and eat and drink, but be not extravagant [7:31].

The Qur'ān describes pious believers as "those who, when they spend, are neither prodigal nor grudging; and there is even a firm station between the two [25:67]." When the Prophet overheard some men speaking, each describing the way in which he had decided to pursue an ascetic life, the Prophet emerged from his room and told them:

> Are you the group one of whom vowed to stay up worshipping all night time every night for ever, and another undertook to fast every day for the rest of his life and the third vowed to avoid women and never get married? As for me, I worship part of the night and rest the other part; I fast some days and do not fast the other days; and I do not keep away from women. This is my customary practice. Whoever deviates from it is not one of us.[10]

The Prophet also advised: "The worst vessel the son of Adam can fill to capacity is his stomach. Even if he wishes to do so, let him fill one third with food, leaving one third for his drink and one third for his breath."[11]

Returning to the question of the economic drive behind the individual's efforts to achieve his own self-interest, we may reiterate that Islam holds that pursuit to be praiseworthy. The motive of self-interest agrees with God's design for the world, and its success at least relieves society of the burden of carrying the cost of an individual's living as well as that of his dependents. An individual may also contribute to the total national production. There is greater merit, however, if the worker also intends by his efforts, in addition to gaining wealth, to give himself the opportunity to be charitable, thereby accumulating rewards with God in Paradise. According to the Qur'ān, "Those who spend their wealth by night and day, by stealth and openly, verily their reward is with their Lord, and they shall suffer neither fear nor grief [2:274]." "God blights usury and causes charity to expand [2:276]."

The motive of working to provide for others—that is, to increase productivity—is praised in Islam, as the following *hadīths* (traditions) tell us:

Whosoever plants a tree, from the fruit of which a bird, a human being or an animal eats, will be recorded for him as a charity.[12]

Whosoever revives a piece of dead land, it becomes his own property.[13]

If one of you should start planting a small tree, let him finish his job even if he should be startled by the disasters of the Day of Judgment.[14]

Such is the Islamic emphasis on the merits of efforts to increase the production of needed goods, not only through agriculture but also through other means, such as fishing, manufacturing, and animal husbandry. Not only did the Prophet praise earning from the labor of the hand, but he also commended the vocation of the shepherd, saying: "God never sent a Messenger except that he had had the experience of working as a shepherd for a time."[15] The Prophet also urged perfecting manufactured goods[16] and advocated fair and prompt payment of the wages due for labor: "Pay a worker his wages before his sweat dries."[17] In some other traditions, the Prophet recommended that wages should be adequate as to meet the costs of food, housing, transportation, and marriage expenses if the worker is not yet married.[18]

The motive of seeking to accumulate wealth for its own sake or for the sake of greater security, though morally it is not counted among the higher category of motives, is not regarded as a sin so long as it does not lead to prohibited practices such as gambling and trading in liquor and provided that alms are duly given. The danger arises when the accumulation of wealth becomes the focus of attention, because then God and the desire to serve Him are no longer central. A person drowning in a sea of materialism may also be subtly trapped into making serious errors and be distracted from other duties. Moreover, focusing on materialism this way is immoderate. As the Qur'ān therefore warns:

> O you who believe! Let not your wealth or your children distract you from remembrance of God. Those who do so are indeed the losers [64:9].

> Your wealth and your children are only sources of temptation; whereas God! with Him there is an immense reward [64:15].

> Wealth and children are an ornament of life of this world. Yet, the good deeds which endure are better in the sight of your Lord for reward, and better in respect of hope [18:46].

> Know that life in this world is only play and idle talk and pageantry and boasting among you and rivalry of wealth and children. [It is] like vegetation after rain, whereof the growth is pleasing to the husbandmen, but afterward it dries up and you see it turn yellow, then it becomes straw [57:2].

> Indeed life of this world is but a passing comfort, and the Hereafter is verily the enduring abode [40:39].

The Prophet said that "Whosoever makes accumulation of wealth the ultimate aim of his life, God will make the spectre of poverty ever-present in front of his eyes."[19] "Should the son of Adam get in his possession so much gold as to fill a wide valley, he will still crave for more!"[20]

In summary, Islam does not regard the accumulation of wealth in itself as a blameworthy pursuit, even when the motive is the individual's craving for greater security or his desire to improve his worldly material condition. The only stipulation, as indicated earlier, is that wealth should be earned through lawful, honest means and that the alms due to the poor are fully paid. The only danger is when the craving for wealth turns into greed and selfishness.

The value of wealth lies in what wealth can purchase. Its best investment is in storing it with God. The following words are from the Qur'ān:

> The likeness of those who spend their wealth in the way of God is as the likeness of a grain which grows seven ears, in each ear there are one hundred grains [2:261].

> Who is it, who is prepared to lend God a good loan which

God will return in multiple rewards. . . . On the day when you can see the believing men and the believing women with their light preceding them; [and it will be said unto them]: Here is a good tiding for you, gardens in Paradise under which the rivers flow. Therein they reside forever. Lo! This is indeed the great success! [57:11]

And pay the poor due, and [so] lend unto God a goodly loan. Whatever good you send before your souls, you will surely find it with God better and greater in recompense [73:20].

The Prophet said:

No matter how much wealth you may accumulate, you gain from it only what you eat, which perishes; and what you dress, which wears away; and what you pay in charity, which lasts for you! That which remains will only benefit your heirs![21]

Three things follow a dead person on his journey to his grave: his family, his wealth, and his work. As soon as he is laid to rest in his grave, his family and his wealth forsake him, and only his work will remain with him in his grave![22]

The Prophet's praise of payment in charity caused the poor among his Companions to complain to him, "Those of means will alone enjoy the rewards for charity!" The Prophet comforted them: "There is indeed a charity in saying a word praising God. And every thanksgiving word is a charity. Repeating the word of *tawhīd* [monotheism] is a charity. Removing an object blocking the way is a charity. And helping your brother lift his burden is a charity."[23]

Wealth, however, is to be earned legitimately, by either work or trade or received as a gift or as a share in an inheritance. Islam regards work, including manual work, as a noble and honorable pursuit that is pleasing to God. The Holy Qur'ān says:

And say [unto them]: Work! God will behold your work, and so will His Messenger and the believers. And you will be brought back before the One Who knows the invisible and the visible worlds, and He will tell you what you used to do [9:105].

Whosoever undertakes good work, male or female, and is a believer, him We shall verily quicken with good life, and We shall pay them a recompense in proportion to the best of what they used to do [16:97].

One day, while the Prophet was sitting in his mosque, a man came up and asked him for a charity. The Prophet [who apparently had noth-

9

ing to give] asked the beggar: "Do you have anything at home?" The man said, "Yes, only a garment of which we spread one part [to sleep on] and cover ourselves with the other part. We also have a pot from which we drink." The Prophet asked the beggar to bring those articles, and he did. Then the Prophet asked those present: "Who is prepared to purchase these two articles?" One Companion offered to purchase them for one dirham. The Prophet then asked whether anyone else would be willing to buy them for two dirhams? Someone paid two dirhams for the articles, and the Prophet gave the money to the beggar, telling him to buy food for himself and his wife with one dirham and to buy an ax with the other dirham. When the man brought the ax, the Prophet himself fixed a handle for it, gave it back to the man, and told him to go and cut wood with the ax and not to return for fifteen days. The man went away, cut wood, and sold it and then returned to the Prophet in fifteen days, having earned ten dirhams, with which he bought food and clothing. The Prophet told him:

> This is better for you than coming on the day of judgment before God to account for your deeds with a blemish in your face caused by begging. Begging is lawful only to one who is a helpless destitute, or burdened with heavy debt [immediately due] or has to pay a heavy blood money in his endeavor to settle disputes and stop bloodshedding.[24]

The Prophet also said:

> The most blessed sustenance is that which one earns through the labor of one's own hand.[25]

> Whoever goes to bed exhausted because of hard work, he has thereby caused his sins to be absolved.[26]

> It is better for a person to take his rope, pick up woods, tie them up, carry them on his back and sell them, than humiliating himself by asking others to give him charity. They may give and may not.[27]

Trade is especially endorsed and praised. According to the Holy Qur'ān:

> O you who believe! Squander not your wealth among yourselves in vanity, except it be a trade by mutual consent, and kill not one another. . . . And who so does that through aggression and injustice, We shall cast him into Fire, and that is even easy for God! [4:29–30]

> And we have settled you firmly on the earth, and have appointed for you therein livelihood [7:10].

He [God] it is Who has made the earth subservient to you, so walk around in its paths [travelling], and seek your provision from His Providence [67:15].

The Prophet said:

An honest true tradesman will be [in Heaven] with the Prophets and the choice of righteous people and the martyrs.[28]

Travel [seeking your provision], you will earn satisfaction.[29]

A hand that gives is better than the hand which takes.[30]

'Umar the second caliph, preached:

Let not any of you lazily make no efforts to earn his living and yet keep praying: "O God! Bring me my sustenance!" Heaven does not rain gold or silver pieces, and the Almighty God commands [in the Holy Qur'ān]: And when the prayer session is over, disperse on the earth and seek [your sustenance] from the bounties of the Almighty.[31]

The redistribution of wealth is ensured in various ways: through the Islamic institution of zakat, the emphasis on the payment of charities over and above the prescribed amounts of the zakat, the financial obligation toward one's kin, and the mechanism of inheritance. The zakat is an annual obligatory payment of 2½ percent of accumulated savings remaining in one's possession for a year. The same applies to commercial goods: 2½ percent of the lowest total value of those goods during the year is to be paid as the zakat. One-fifth, however, is due from any excavated pre-Islamic treasure found on one's own property. The same is true in the case of extracted minerals. One-tenth of agricultural produce is due as soon as it has been harvested. If effort went into irrigation of the land, however, only half of one-tenth is due.[32]

Whether the zakat payment is made to the state, as it should be, or given directly to the poor, it is a manifestation of social solidarity among the believers in Islam and a means of reducing the hardships of the poor. It generates good will on the part of the poor toward the rich. Above all, the payment represents humble obedience to God. The zakat is the third pillar of Islam, the other four being a confession of faith in the Islamic creed, performing the five daily prayers at prescribed times, fasting during the lunar month (Ramadan), and making a pilgrimage to Mecca at least once in a lifetime. The zakat also prompts the possessor of money to invest his wealth— otherwise, the zakat payment will eat it up. Thus, the Prophet taught that the wealth of an orphan should be invested for him by his guardian "so that it will not be eaten up by the zakat."[33] Saving and investing are not frowned on in Islam. On the contrary, said the Prophet, "To leave your dependents well off is better than leaving them in need, compelled to stretch out their hands in charity."[34]

The emphasis placed on paying the zakat is reflected in many passages of the Holy Qur'ān. The zakat giver is praised and promised great rewards, and payment of the zakat is commanded. Those who fail to pay it are warned:

> Keep up saying the prayer and give away the zakat [2:43, 83, 110; 22:78; 24:65; 73:20].
>
> And woe unto the polytheists, who do not pay the zakat . . . [41:6–7].
>
> Especially those who are diligent in prayers and those who pay the zakat, the believers in God and the Last Day. Upon them We shall bestow immense reward [4:162].

The Prophet said:

> Whosoever has been blessed by God with wealth and fails to pay its zakat his wealth will come on the Day of Judgment, like a giant bold snake with two red spots over the eyes, and encircle him, and holding his jaw, will say to him: "I am your wealth, I am your hoarded treasure."[35]

The Prophet then recited the Qur'ān [3:180]: "Let not those who hoard up that which God has bestowed upon them of His bounty think that it is better for them. Nay, it is worse for them. That which they hoard up will be their collar on the Day of Judgment." The Prophet also said:

> No people withhold payment of zakat except that God will visit them with famine. Were it not for their cattle they would not get any rain.[36]
>
> Whenever the zakat mixes with wealth [because of not being paid off] it causes it corruption.[37]
>
> Whoever pays it [the zakat] voluntarily for God's sake, will receive God's reward for it; but I shall take it by force from those who dare to withhold it, and impose a fine upon them, half of their wealth, nothing of theirs should be for the benefit of the family of Muhammad.[38]
>
> And tell them [the Prophet told Muadh, one of his Companions when he sent him as his viceroy over the Yemen] that God has made it [the zakat] obligatory: a payment to be made by the rich among them to the poor; but insist not

upon the best quality and you should fear the effect of the prayer of the oppressed. There is no obstruction on its way to God.[39]

A Muslim must also pay the cost of living of his wife, whether she is rich or poor, and the cost of maintaining his children—the male till the age of puberty and the female till marriage—his needy parents, grandparents, and siblings. One must also extend help to distant relatives and to needy neighbors. The Holy Qur'ān reads:

> And serve God. Ascribe no partnership to Him. Show kindness toward your parents and unto your kindred and the orphans and the needy and unto the near neighbor who is also of kin [unto you] and the neighbor who is not of kin and the fellow traveler and the wayfarer and those in your possession [4:36].

> Give your kin his due, the poor and the needy and the wayfarer . . . [17:26].

The Prophet said:

> Whoever truly believes in God let him keep the rope tying him to his relatives by being helpful to them.[40]

> A blood relation is hanging by the side of the Throne [of God], saying, God will keep the tie of him who keeps me, and will abandon him who dares to break me.[41]

> [Do good to] your mother and your father and your sister and your brother and to him who deserves your loyalty. [This is] an obligatory duty and a link with kindred which has to be maintained.[42]

> The best you may consume is that which you earn through your labor. Your children are the fruit of your efforts, therefore [whatever you get through them is lawful, so] consume it happily in good health.[43]

> Start with yourself [that is, seek first to satisfy your own needs], then those who are your dependents, then those who are your other kin . . . the nearer, then the next.[44]

> "They belong to me [spiritually] and I belong to them," the Prophet spoke praising the Ash'arite tribe of the Yemen, because, he said, "In time of hardship, they pooled together all food they possessed for their common benefit, sharing it equally."[45]

> By God, he is not a true believer, he who goes to bed with a full stomach while his neighbor is hungry![46]

My brother Gabriel urged me concerning the duties due to a neighbor so persistently that I thought he nearly made him an heir with a share in the estate![47]

According to the Shari'a law of Islam, the estate of a deceased person, man or woman, should be distributed among his heirs, who include all the surviving children, the surviving spouse, and the surviving parent(s). In the absence of a male child of direct descent and in the absence of the father of the deceased person, his grandfather, brothers, and sisters may inherit a share. In some cases, his brother's son and his father's brother and the latter's son may also inherit a share in the absence of a more closely related person.[48] The special situations in which each person may inherit a share, and the determination of the size of the share due to each, are too complex for a full discussion here. In the absence of the specified categories of heirs, however, some other relatives may claim a share.[49]

This brief explanation of the Islamic mechanism of inheritance demonstrates not only how Islam has sought to achieve justice among members of the extended family but also how its method protects against the concentration of wealth and resources in the hands of a few. Islam also inspires social cohesion among members of each extended family and reduces the causes of jealousy and social tension.

By now, readers will have gained a sense of how much Islam emphasizes charity above and beyond the payment of the zakat and the obligations owed relatives and neighbors. Let us quote some relevant texts:

The likeness of those who spend their wealth in the way of God is as the likeness of a grain which grows seven ears, each ear bears one hundred grains [2:261].

Beautified for mankind is love of pleasures [that comes] from women and offspring, and stored up heaps of gold and silver, and horses branded [with their mark], and cattle and land. All this is comfort of the life of this world. God! With Him is a more excellent abode. Say: shall I inform of something better than that? For those who keep away from evil, with their Lord, are Gardens underneath which rivers flow, and in which they reside forever, and pure companions and contentment from God [3:14–15].

Believe in God and His Messenger and spend of that whereof He has made you trustees; and such of you as believe and spend, there will be a great reward [57:7].

Who is he who will lend unto God a goodly loan, that He may double it for him, and his may be a rich reward? [57:11].

It is not righteous that you turn your face to the east or the west; but righteous is he who believes in God and the Last Day and the Angels and the Scripture and the Prophets; and give his wealth for love of Him [God], to kinsfolk, to the orphans, to the needy, to the wayfarer and to those who ask, and to the cause of freeing the slaves; and observes proper worship and pays the poor due . . . [2:177].

Nay, but you honor not the orphan, and urge not each other to feed the poor [89:17–18].

And we did not feed the poor [74:44]. [Those condemned to the Hellfire regrettably give this as one of the reasons of their punishment.]

And whatever you spend [for a good cause] He [God] replaces, and He is the best of the Providers [34:39].

And vie with one another for your Lord's forgiveness and for a Paradise as wide as are the heavens and the earth, prepared for those who ward off [evil], those who spend [of that which God has given them] in ease and in adversity . . . [3:133–34].

The Prophet also said:

Protect against the punishment of the Hellfire by paying a charity, even as small as one half of a date.[50]

Every person, on the Day of Judgment when the sun becomes very close to people, will be in the shade of his charity, until the process of Hisab [each person giving account to God] is over.[51]

A person runs after his wealth, screaming: "My wealth! My wealth!" Yet, in fact, a person gets of his wealth only what he consumes, which in fact is of short value; what he wears, and it fades away; and what he gives away in charity, which lasts for him. That which remains is left for use by others.[52]

A charity extinguishes [eliminates] the evils of sins as much as water extinguishes fire.[53]

Believers to each other are like the bricks of a building, which hold to each other.[54]

The believers in their mutual love, sympathy and cooperation, are like the [interacting] parts of the human body: when one part complains, the other parts call each other to hasten to its rescue, each sharing its pain and sleeplessness.[55]

The annals of Islam tell very inspiring stories about the amazing charities of the early Muslim generations. In reading such literature

15

one gets the impression that those early Muslims behaved as if they could see with their naked eyes the indescribable rewards awaiting charitable people in Paradise![56] It is important, however, to add that not only is charity urged toward deserving persons of the same faith, but sympathy is also owed to neighbors and needy persons of other religions. Abdullah Ibn Umar, a celebrated companion of the Prophet, used to tell his servant repeatedly when he slaughtered a sheep, "Remember our Jewish neighbor."[57] And his father, the renowned second caliph, Umar, having seen an old Jewish person begging in the streets of Medina, called him and asked him to rest. He told him, "We have not been fair to you. We collected your taxes when you were young and abandoned you when you became old." He then ordered that his full maintenance be met by the treasury.[58]

These remarks demonstrate the individual's social responsibility and the Islamic communal solidarity. So the individual must harmonize his own needs with social responsibilites, and his material aspirations with his spiritual obligations.

In keeping with the Islamic belief in promoting productive practices, Islam condemns all disruptive and unproductive activities. Gambling, games of chance, trading in liquor, theft, extortion, highway robbery, hoarding, cheating, monopoly, usury, and the financial exploitation of sex are included in the list of grave sins.[59] From its inception, Islam has emphasized what is called, in modern terminology, basic human rights. These rights include not only the respect for human life and dignity owed every human being, but also the principle of individual liberty and the protection of private property as well as the provision of equal opportunity and justice for all, without discrimination on the basis of descent, nationality, color, wealth, or sex.[60] They also include the right to learn, the right to earn, and the right to own the fruit of one's own labor. Respecting and protecting private property, together with protecting human life, were categorically stipulated in the treaty concluded by the Prophet with the tribal chiefs in Medina, including those of the Jewish tribes then living in that town.[61] The same terms were reiterated in covenants subsequently concluded by the caliphs.[62] So, no mortal has the right to confiscate or to interfere with the property of someone else. Yet, man's ownership of property, movable or immovable, is temporary; property is a borrowed possession.[63] Man's ownership of property is indeed merely a trusteeship. God Himself is the real owner. "To Him alone belongs all that is in heaven and all that is in the earth and all that is between them, and all that is under the earth [20:6]."

Man's awareness of this dual ownership—or, rather, of his trusteeship on behalf of God in God's own property—inspires him to use care and caution. He realizes his responsibility in the manner in which he dispenses with wealth. He will not waste it or abuse it. He will only put it to good use.

One of the great achievements of Islam was the liberation of the human person. In Mecca, the aristocratic class exploited its position as custodian of the Ka'ba (the central religious shrine for all Arabia), which it surrounded with idols, and mistreated women and the poor strata of society. Beginning early in the 7th century A.D., Islam eradicated these injustices and proclaimed the full equality of mankind:

> O you people! We have indeed created you all from one male and one female, and have made you nations and tribes only in order to know each other. Verily the noblest of you in the eyes of God are those of best conduct [Qur'ān, 49:13].

> All people are equal, as equal as the teeth of a comb. No white may claim preference over a black, nor an Arab over a non-Arab. Only piety [and good deeds] count.[64]

> Your brothers are your servants. Feed them from what you eat, dress them from the same quality of your own clothes, and do not charge them with a burden beyond their ability; if you should do, you must assist them.[65]

Deeply offended by these humane teachings, the arrogant Arabs reproached Muhammad: "Do you want us to treat our slaves and our women as equal to us?" Their opposition to Islam was a rejection of both its pure, uncompromising monotheism and its social reforms. Thirteen years of Muslims' perseverance in the face of severe persecution in Mecca and then eight years of armed conflict after Muhammad's emigration to Medina forced Mecca to capitulate to Islam. Subsequently, all Arabia was unified under the banner of Islam, and the new state was consolidated through the Islamic ideals of justice, equality, and individual liberty. Firm social solidarity was brought about through the bond of Islam.

Individual liberty has to be tempered by wisdom that acknowledges the liberty of others and harmonizes one's own self-interests with those of society. Enlightened personal liberty adjusts one's own self-interest with that of the community, since a community's best interests consist of the sum of the real best interests of the members of the community. When this total is hurt, the interests of some members will also be hurt.

Yet in trying to achieve their economic best interests, people often become blinded to the best interests of others. Their judgment cannot always be objective, and thus they often step out of bounds. There has to be a corrective hand having the power of coercion, so

17

that violations can be corrected and rechanneled into a permissible orbit. The state has such a powerful hand, and therefore the state has the right—indeed, the obligation and the function—to keep an eye on the dynamics of the national economy and to take measures to ensure its safety and soundness.

When the Prophet emigrated from Mecca and settled in Medina in 622 A.D., setting up the embryonic Muslim state, he found out that there was only one marketplace, which was inside the territory of a Jewish tribe (called Banu Qaynuqa') who imposed heavy tolls on the Arabs who used it. So the Prophet built a tent nearby to serve as another market and ordered that there should be no tolls or hardship or hoarding of foodstuffs. In a fit of anger, Ka'b Ibn al-Ashraf, the chief of the tribe, destroyed the tent. Under the circumstances, the Prophet moved his market to another site, again ordering that there should be no tolls imposed on those who used the market and no hoarding of foodstuffs.[66] From time to time, the Prophet inspected the market. In a celebrated tradition we are told that on one such visit to the market, he dipped his hand into a pile of grains. Although the top layer of the grain looked good and clean, the Prophet took out a handful of wet grain. The trader said that it had been hit by rain, but the Prophet retorted, "Whosoever cheats us is not one of us."[67] One of the Prophet's measures to ensure the smooth running of the market-place was to prohibit the practice of intercepting farmers on their way to the market to purchase their goods at prices not comparable to those of the market.[68]

These traditions illustrate the responsibility that those in author-ity have toward the health of the communal economy. This responsi-bility should be limited, fair, and wise, taking into account all factors. We are told, for example, that when the prices of goods went up, it was suggested that the Prophet order them lowered. According to the story, the Prophet declined the suggestion, saying: "It is God Who gives sustenance; sometimes widely and sometimes narrowly."[69] Nevertheless, some leading jurists hold that governments should en-force fair prices, especially in times of crises.[70] Apparently, the Prophet felt that the rise of prices at the time was justified and that it was not exorbitant.

Thus, the state must keep a watchful eye on the economy to ensure justice and maintain its soundness. This should be a beneficent supervision, the weight of which should not be felt ad-versely by the complying individual who is already bound morally by Islam. Such supervision should reflect that morality, respect personal economic liberty, provide measures that are conducive to economic success, and only intervene to prevent violations.

18

Let us now sum up the preceding discussion to convey in a nutshell the Islamic concept of economics:

- Economics in Islam is a moral doctrine, based on Islamic religious values derived from Qur'ānic guidance. This religious warmth, unlike scientific coolness provides healthy fuel to economic action, adding to the natural drive of serving self-interests. At the same time, the religious conscience protects against corrupt practices. Although the concept of Islamic economics is based on revelation, it appeals to intellectual reflection and complies with human needs.

- Being both spiritual and practical, the Islamic economic system seeks to find a middle way that avoids the extremes of meanness and extravagance and that strives to fulfill the needs of the soul and those of the body.

- Besides its short-term objective—namely, to serve human earthly needs and to provide material satisfaction and relative earthly happiness—the Islamic system of economics has a long-term objective: to seek to earn God's pleasure and gain His rewards in Paradise. So, it is not simply a materialistic system.[71]

- The concept of the dual ownership of personal property is one of the special features of the Islamic doctrine of economics. Islam protects and endorses the personal right to own what one may freely gain, through legitimate means, such as gifts and the fruits of the labor of one's hand or intellect. It is a sacred right.[72] Yet, human ownership is tempered by the understanding that everything, in the last analysis, belongs to God, including our souls and bodies, as well as the means of our living, which God has created for our benefit. What appears to be ownership is in fact a matter of trusteeship, whereby we have temporary authority to handle and benefit from property, which will change hands on death.

- The Islamic doctrine of economics involves both citizens and the state in a pattern of partnership that inspires a deep sense of communal responsibility. Although Islam endorses and protects and even demands individual liberty, it makes a clear distinction between economic liberty and greed. Economic liberty, according to its definition, recognizes and harmonizes with the liberty of others, and adjusts to communal needs and interests. This entails two things: One is an obligation on the part of the state to keep watch from a distance and to do everything to promote prosperity and hinder adversity.[73] The other is a special obligation on the part of successful citizens who make a surplus above the needs of themselves and their dependents, to invest that surplus in helping those in need. The Prophet taught that "whoever has an additional riding beast let him help him who does not have one, and whoever has some surplus food should extend it to him who does not have food."[74] In case of failure, the state has to intervene and take from the rich to give to the poor.

- The Islamic system of economics is comprehensive in that it pays attention to all aspects of the economic process. It stimulates production, insists on fair distribution, and calls for moderation in consumption. Islam honors both work and trade. To provide for fair distribution, it has made payment of the zakat and almsgiving cardinal obligations, and the support of close kin a duty. It has widened the circle of one's heirs and prohibits favoring one child over another.[75] Islam also condemns the vice of overeating[76] and extravagant practices.[77] It calls for moderation.[78] It even teaches its adherents to eat slowly, to take small morsels, and to take sips of water when drinking.[79] It forbids the consumption of liquor and the flesh of swine and all harmful things.[80]

- The Islamic system of economics, which gives equal attention to both the individual and his community, lays emphasis on the immediate personal motive, unlike systems that only stress the ultimate result for the community. Islam does not merge the individual into the community, nor does it ignore his social obligations. Islam sees no conflict between the legitimate interests of the individual and those of his community. Disregarding immediate personal motives and stressing only the ultimate outcome for the community has led to greed, selfishness, and unspeakable suffering. Paying equal attention to immediate personal motives and at the same time insisting that those motives should be agreeable are ways to guide human economic liberty toward a harmony between the best interests of the individual and those of society. The outcome, in this way, will be better and greater.

- The Islamic economic system is both flexible and rigid. It is flexible because it largely consists of general guidelines, such as the teaching that urges productive hard work, the call to consume useful things and avoid what may be harmful,[81] and the sanction to enjoy all God's favors not only in meeting basic needs but also in seeking recreational activities.[82] Thus the teaching that praises hard work can be realized by engaging in any profitable activity. That honoring commerce can be achieved by trading in groceries, clothing, grain, or electronics. Edible food can be any dish, and harmful things to be avoided include poison and liquor and harmful drugs. Again, work can be manual or mental. Trade can be in such simple goods as wool and hides, as well as in other goods such as automobiles and houses. The dynamism of Islam, which was still confined to the sands of Arabia at the time of the death of the Prophet in A.D. 632 but spread extensively within a decade, has enabled it to meet and adjust to the

20

needs of this expansion which brought within its fold ancient nations with different cultures and civilizations.

Yet, the Islamic system is characterized by a degree of ridigity that maintains its character and gives it its Islamic trademark, so to speak. The framework of Islamic economics is held together by a set of specific ordinances established within the lifetime of the Prophet and now not subject to modification. These include the peculiarly Islamic obligation of zakat, the specific financial obligations incumbent upon an individual toward members of his kin, the way in which the estate of a deceased person has to be distributed, the prohibition of hoarding and all usurious practices, and the special pattern of economic relationships between citizens and the authorities as explained earlier. The Islamic system also prohibits all income gained through illegal practices such as gambling or trading in liquor or in sex or pornography. The Prophet said, "Any piece of human flesh nourished by illegal earning will burn in the Hellfire."[83] Therefore, Muslims are careful not to consume anything resulting from a doubtful source. (Islam, however, shares with other systems the proscription against theft, extortion, cheating, and fraud.)

The preceding discourse describes the ideal, not necessarily the practice. One must make a distinction between that ideal and the reality, and between Muslims in the ideal and Muslims as they actually behave. There is often a gap between the ideal and its application. It is similar to the difference between the Christian ideal and a member of the Christian faith. Injustice, corruption, and bloodletting have been committed in the name of a faith that teaches love, tenderness, and sympathy. Similarly, there is and has almost always been a gap between Islam and the Muslims. This gap has varied throughout the past fourteen centuries, the age of the Islamic religion. It was almost nonexistent during the life of the Prophet and the reigns of his two immediate caliphs. For nearly thirty years, Islam was indeed an ideal society. Its ideals of justice, love, devotion, and respect for the Islamic virtues and teachings were meticulously observed. Then the gap between the ideal and practice began to emerge and slowly grew wider. At times it narrowed and then grew. In the glorious moments when the gap narrowed, Islam nearly eliminated poverty. Government agents in some regions could not find a poor person to be paid zakat funds. They had to dispense with it by purchasing slaves in order to set them free![84]

The gap separating Muslims from the ideal of Islam's economic doctrine widened considerably when the Muslim world fell under European occupation and when the colonial masters replaced traditional Muslim systems with their own legal and economic institutions. This unhappy situation lasted far too long and caused deep stagnation and the spreading of ignorance and poverty. When Muslims at last recovered and their sovereignty was restored to them in recent years, they found their economy entangled in a banking system based on usurious practices. For decades they had to tolerate the alien system. Many of them hesitated to invest their surplus funds in these banks against their religious consciences. After strenuous effort, research, and experimentation, several Muslim experts developed a new genre of financial institution, the Islamic bank. The experiment in Dubai, in the United Arab Emirates, in March 1975, and its early success led to a proliferation of Islamic banks in a number of Muslim capitals.

The main feature of the Islamic bank is the absence of a fixed rate of interest. The investor accepts the risk of loss, though loss is hardly expected. The system is therefore based on profit sharing, not on interest. The bank invests the funds of its depositors and shareholders directly in profitable projects or helps finance sound projects of Muslim entrepreneurs. The profits gained from these activities are shared by the bank and the investors. The bank may also lend money for sound projects for a reasonable service charge.[85]

It remains to be seen how successful this venture will be. The profits gained by investors in these banks, according to this writer's knowledge are much less than the interest currently paid to investors by traditional banks. Nevertheless, one has to make allowances for such young institutions. Time and experience might improve circumstances, and current rates of interest are obviously inflated.

What disturbs this writer is that some of these Islamic banks seem to be engaging in some sort of roundabout method to circumvent the prohibition against usury. The business of paying and taking a fixed interest is subtly yet certainly involved, as for example in selling a commodity at a price higher than the market price to customers who pay in installments. The banks claim that this practice is a lawful sale, not usury, since no fixed interest is specifically stated.[86] This defense, in the writer's view, is not convincing.

Notes

1. Abu al-Su'ud, *Tafsir* [Qur'ānic exegesis] (Cairo, 1928), p. 634. Cf. Isma'il al-'Ajluni, *Kashf al-Khafa wa Muzil al-Iltibas* (Cairo, n.d.), vol. 2, p. 132.

2. Muslim Ibn al-Hajjaj, *Sahih* (with commentary by Imam al-Nawawi) (Beirut, 1978), vol. 13, pp. 53–54.

3. Ibid., vol. 2, pp. 147–50. Cf. Bukhari, *Sahih*, Halabi (Cairo, 1951), vol. 14, pp. 106–12.

4. Bukhari, *Sahih*, vol. 15, pp. 207 ff.

5. Ibid., vol. 11, p. 85. In the last analysis, these three things, including the coming into being of one's own child, can be attributed to a person's own efforts.

6. Ahmad Ibn Ali, better known as Al-Khatib al-Baghdadi, *Ta'rikh* [*History of*] *Baghdad*, Sa'adah Press, Cairo 1931, vol. VII, pp. 342–43.

7. Ibid.

8. See chapter 73, verse 20. 'Umar Ibn al-Khattab, the renowned second caliph, is supposed to have said: "I would prefer dying while struggling for my sustenance and the sustenance of my children, to dying while fighting in the defense of the faith." He then referred to this Qur'ānic verse to support his words. According to the *Shari'a* law of Islam, it is obligatory to struggle to earn the means to supply the basic needs of oneself and one's family. To work to earn more is considered to be of greater merit than engaging in supererogatory worship. Ref. Shaikh Abd al-Hayy al-Kattani, *Kitab Nizam al-Hukumah al-Nabawiyyah*, also known as *Al-Taratib al-Idariyyah* [System of the prophetic government] (Beirut, A.H. 1347), vol. 2, pp. 3 and 24, respectively.

9. Abu Hamid Al-Ghazzali, *Ihya' 'Ulum al-Din* [Revival of the sciences of religion] (Cairo, n.d.), vol. 2, p. 56.

10. Muslim, *Sahih*, vol. 9, pp. 175–76.

11. Ahmad Ibn Hanbal, *Al-Musnad* (Cairo, 1933), vol. 4, p. 132.

12. Muslim, *Sahih*, vol. 10, p. 213. Cf. *Al-Musnad*, vol. 2, p. 147.

13. *Al-Musnad*, vol. 3, pp. 204, 256.

14. Ibid., vol. 3, pp. 184, 191.

15. Ibn Majah, *Sunan* (Cairo, 1954), vol. 2, p. 727.

16. Al-'Ajluni, *Kashf al-Khafa*, vol. 1, p. 426.

17. Ibn Majah, *Sunan*, vol. 2, p. 817.

18. Abu Dawud Sulaiman Ibn al-Ash'ath, *Sunan* (Beirut: Dar al-Fikr, n.d.), vol. 3, p. 135.

19. Ibn Majah, *Sunan*, vol. 2, p. 1375.

20. Muslim, *Sahih*, vol. 7, pp. 138–39.

21. Ibid., vol. 4, pp. 24, 26; vol. 18, p. 94.

22. Muslim, *Sahih*, vol. 18, p. 95.

23. Ibid., vol. 4, p. 223; *Al-Musnad*, vol. 5, pp. 167–68.

24. Ibn Majah, *Sunan*, vol. 2, pp. 740–41.

25. *Al-Musnad*, vol. 2, pp. 334, 357. This teaching occurred in different styles and is quoted in various sources.

26. Al-Gazzali, *Ihya'*, vol. 2, p. 81.

27. Ibid., vol. 1, pp. 164, 167. Nasa'i, *Sunan*, vol. 2, pp. 70–71.

28. Tirmidhi, *Sunan* (Beirut: Dar al-Fikr, n.d.), vol. 2, p. 341.

29. *Al-Musnad*, vol. 2, p. 280.

30. Muslim, *Sahih*, vol. 7, pp. 124–27; Nasa'i, *Sunan*, vol. 2, p. 45.

31. Al-Kattani, *Al-Taratib al-Idariyyah*, vol. 2, p. 23.

32. Muhammad Abdul-Rauf, *Islam, Faith and Devotion* (Lagos, Nigeria, 1972), pp. 103ff.

33. Cf. *Al-Fiqh Ala 'l-Madhahib Al-Arba'ah* [The Shari'a law according to the four schools of law] (Cairo: Ministry of Endowments, 1939), vol. 1, p. 492ff.

34. Ibn Majah, *Sunan*, vol. 2, p. 904.

35. Muslim, *Sahih*, vol. 7, p. 70; Nasa'i, *Sunan*, vol. 2, p. 8.

36. Ibn Majah, *Sunan*, vol. 2, p. 22.

37. Al-'Ajluni, *Kashf al-Khafa*, vol. 2, p. 188.

38. Nasa'i, *Sunan*, vol. 2, p. 11.

39. Ibid., vol. 2, p. 3. Muslim, *Sahih*, vol. 1, pp. 195–97. Bukhari, *Al-Jami' al-Sahih* (with commentary by Ibn Hajar al-'Asqalani) (Cairo: Halabi Press, 1951), vol. 18, pp. 115–16.

40. Muslim, *Sahih*, vol. 2, pp. 18–20.

41. Ibid., vol. 2, p. 113.

42. Abu Dawud, *Sunan*, vol. 4, p. 336.

43. Nasa'i, *Sunan*, vol. 7, p. 212.

44. Ibid., pp. 52–53; Muslim, *Sahih*, vol. 7, pp. 125–27.

45. Muhammad Al-Mubarak, *Nizam Al-Islam: Al-Iqtisad* [The economic system in Islam] (Beirut, 1978), p. 134.

46. *Al-Musnad*, vol. 1, p. 55.

47. Muslim, *Sahih*, vol. 15, p. 176.

48. Qur'ān, chap. 4, verses 11, 12, 176.

49. Abdullah Ibn Ahmad, better known as Al-Nasafi, *Tafsir* [*Exegesis of*] *Al-Qur'ān* (Beirut, n.d.), vol. 1, pp. 208–13 and 267–68. For further details, chapters on inheritance in Muslim legal texts can be consulted.

50. Muslim, *Sahih*, vol. 7, pp. 100–102.

51. *Al-Musnad*, vol. 4, p. 148.

52. Muslim, *Sahih*, vol. 18, p. 94.

53. *Al-Musnad*, vol. 2, p. 321; vol. 5, p. 348.

54. Muslim, *Sahih*, vol. 16, p. 139.

55. Bukhari, *Sahih* (Beirut, 1978), vol. 4, p. 53; Muslim, *Sahih*, vol. 16, p. 140.

56. Muslim, *Sahih*, vol. 4, p. 223.

57. Abu Dawud, *Sunan*, vol. 4, pp. 338–39.

58. Ya'qub (Abū Yūsūf), *Kitab al-Kharaj* [Book of taxation in Islam], vol. 3, tr. Ben Shemeh and E. J. Brill (London: Leiden and Luzak, 1969), p. 87. This chapter abounds in traditions defending the rights of the People of the Book.

59. Qur'ān, chap. 5, verses 33, 38, 90; chap. 9, verse 35.

60. Qur'ān, chap. 49, verse 13.

61. Tabari, *Ta'rikh* (Cairo: Ma'arif Press, 1970), vol. 2, p. 609; vol. 4, p. 109.

62. Ibid., vol. 4, p. 109.

63. Qur'ān, chap. 57, verse 7; chap. 35, verse 39; chap. 7, verse 128. Man's ownership is likened to a temporary acquisition on behalf of God Who indeed possesses all that is in the heavens and the earth.

64. 'Amr Ibn Bakr Al-Jahiz, *Al-Bayan wa Al-Tabyin* (Cairo: Khanki Press, 1948), vol. 2, p. 19. A classical literary author with immense influence, Al-Jahiz died in 255/869.

65. Muslim, *Sahih*, vol. 11, pp. 132–33; *Al-Musnad*, vol. 5, p. 158.

66. Al-Bahiyy Al-Kholy, *Al-Islam La Shuyu'iyyah Wa La Ra's Maliyyah* [Islam is neither communism nor capitalism] (Cairo, 1956), pp. 60–61.

67. Muslim, *Sahih*, vol. 2, p. 108.

68. Al-Nasa'i, *Sunan*, vol. 7, pp. 224–25.

69. Ibn Majah, *Sunan*, vol. 2, p. 747.

70. Muhammad al-Mubarak, *Nizam al-Iqtisad fi'l-Islam*, pp. 116–18. Cf. M. A. Al-Salih, "Pricing according to Shari'a," *Journal of Islamic Research*, vol. 1, pt. 4, pp. 200–239. Muh. Ibn Sa'ud University, Riyadh.

71. "Seek, in the wealth you have been given by God, success in the Last Abode and do not neglect the share of pleasure in this world you are entitled to; and do good as God has done good to you . . ." (Qur'ān, chap. 28, verse 78). And, according to standard compilations of the *Hadīth*, as reported in Al-'Ajluni, *Kashf Al-Khafa*, the Prophet, peace and blessing be upon him, said: "It is no good to sacrifice this material world thinking it would lead to greater success in the Last Day, nor is it good to indulge in the material pursuit so much so as to neglect working for spiritual success. But one should take from each to the other."

72. The sacred right to own wealth that is earned legitimately is emphasized in the Holy Qur'an, where, as in chapter 2, verse 188, and chapter 4, verse 29, people are warned not to use another's wealth illegitimately but only through lawful transactions and with mutual consent. It is also forbidden to encroach upon the wealth of an orphan (chap. 4, verses 6, 9). The Prophet in his famous speech delivered on Mount 'Arafat during his last pilgrimage, which has become known as the Farewell Speech, declared: "And verily the sacredness of your blood and of your wealth is like the sacredness of this day in this month in this [sacred] town. O Lord! I have conveyed [the message]; please bear witness!" (Ibn Majah, *Sunan*, vol. 2, p. 1296). According to the same author (p. 1297), the Prophet, during his walk around the Ka'ba in Mecca one day, was overheard, by some of his Companions, addressing the Ka'bah: "How good you are! How good is your smell! By God in Whose hand Muhammad's soul is held, the sacredness of the believer, his blood, his wealth and to think well of him, is greater with God, the Almighty." According to Ahmad Ibn Hanbal, in *Al-Musnad*, vol. 5, p. 72, a Companion of the Prophet named Abu Harrah al-Raqqash said that while he was holding the rope of the she-camel that the Prophet was riding during the last days of the farewell pilgrimage, trying to move away the rushing crowds from him, he heard the Prophet asking the thronging crowd: "Do you know what is [the significance of] this day, what is this month, and what is this town?" They answered: "A sacred day, a sacred month and a sacred town." The Prophet then said, "Verily, your blood, your wealth, and your honor are forbidden [to be encroached upon] like the sacredness of this day, and the sacredness of this month and the sacredness of this town until the day you meet with your Lord!" Then he commanded, "Listen carefully. Do not commit injustice. Do not commit injustice. Do not commit injustice! A person's wealth is unlawful unless it is given wholeheartedly." Cf. Bukhari, *Sahih*, vol. 4, p. 57.

73. This *hadīth*, as related by many authorities (for example, by Abu Dawud, *Sunan*, vol. 3, p. 130), says: "Every person is a responsible agent and will be brought to account [before God] and be asked about his responsibilities. Therefore, a ruler is responsible for the well-being of his subjects [citizens] and shall have to give account as to how he discharged this respon-

sibility." The *hadīth* continues to enumerate in the same manner the responsibilities of the husband, the wife, and the servant and concludes "Thus all of you have responsibilities and each shall be asked about his responsibility."

74. *Al-Musnad,*vol. 4, p. 45; Muslim, *Sahih*, vol. 12, p. 33.

75. According to authorities of the *Hadith* (including Muslim, *Sahih*, vol. 11, pp. 65–69, and *Al-Musnad*, vol. 4, pp. 368–70), a Companion of the Prophet went to him along with his own son [who was apparently the child of his favorite wife] and said, "O you the Messenger of God! I have given this son of mine an orchard as a gift and wish that you [the Prophet] would endorse this gift and bear witness for it." The Prophet asked him, "Do you have other children besides him?" "Yes," the man said. The Prophet further inquired, "Have you given each of the other children an equal gift?" "No," came the answer. The Prophet responded, "I do not bear witness for an unjust action."

76. *Al-Musnad*, vol. 4, p. 132.

77. Qur'ān, chap. 7, verse 31; chap. 25, verse 67.

78. Ibid. See also Ibn Hanbal, *Musnad*, vol. 4, p. 132.

79. Tirmidhi, *Sunan*, vol. 2, p. 109; Al-Gazzali, *Al-Ihya'*, vol. 2, pp. 4–5.

80. Qur'ān, chap. 5, verse 90; chap. 6, verse 145; chap. 7, verse 157.

81. Ibid., chap. 2, verse 168; chap. 7, verse 157.

82. Ibid., chap. 7, verses 31–32.

83. *Al-Musnad*, vol. 2, pp. 221, 229; *Al-Ihya'*, vol. 2, p. 6.

84. Yusuf Al-Qaradawi, *Mushkilat al-Faqr wa Kayfa 'Alaja-ha 'l-Islam*, [The problem of poverty and how Islam sought to treat it] (Beirut, 1967), pp. 168–75.

85. Ingo Karsten of the Department of the Middle East, International Monetary Fund, describes the phenomenon of the Islamic banking system as "an integral part of an attempt to move toward the Islamic ideal of a society based on the principle of justice." He also notes that "the profit and loss sharing system (PLS) turns savers into entrepreneurs at least to some extent, by encouraging them to participate directly in the financial success of the investors' business, thereby also sharing the risks involved." He further observes that "the yields to the depositors could be higher under the profit sharing system (PLS), turns savers into entrepreneurs at least to some extent, Made Great Stride, Says IMF," published in *Khaleej Times*, United Arab Emirates, Dubai, March 3, 1982).

86. Muhammad A. Zu'air, "Iftira'at 'ala 'l-Bunuk al-Islamiyyah" [Lies made against the Islamic banks], in *Al-Iqtisad Al-Islami* [The Islamic economics], a journal issued by the Islamic Bank of Dubai, no. 2, (October 1981), pp. 66–67.

2

"The Spirit of Democratic Capitalism": Reflections and Comments

The Islamic concept of economics that we have just formulated must have had a strong hold on the minds of the Muslim generations throughout the fourteen centuries of Islam, guiding them and giving them a sense of direction in their economic activities. Its underlying ideals and values were inculcated in them during their upbringing and sustained, internalized, and reinforced by constant recitation of and listening to the Holy Qur'ān. Repetition of Islamic phrases that convey these values has also had its effect.

I shall now proceed to outline the insights and impressions I have gained from Dr. Novak's book *The Spirit of Democratic Capitalism*,[1] which comprises twenty chapters divided into three parts. In part 1, which consists of nine chapters, the author tries to put into words the structural dynamic beliefs which suffuse the democratic capitalist system. Part 2, which comprises four chapters, "examines what is left of the socialist idea today, so as to glimpse . . . a view of democratic capitalism by contrast." Part 3, which consists of seven chapters, supplies "at least the beginning of a religious perspective on democratic capitalism."

In my long journey through Dr. Novak's volume, and in looking for a theological theory of democratic capitalism, I had to study every page in every chapter in the book. I gained great insight from the author's analysis of the spirit of democratic capitalism. I was particularly impressed by the exposition and explanation of each of the three components of the concept: namely, a democratic polity, a free market and incentive economy, and a moral-cultural system that is pluralistic and liberal. These separate but mutually interdependent institutionalized components are coordinated, cooperating, and converging systems. Economic success depends on this balanced autonomy. Yet, each component needs and depends on the other two.

Democratic capitalism, which developed as a result of the efforts to limit the power of the state and the church, has inspired the notion that capital in itself can expand without causing a loss of wealth to any other party. Democratic capitalism also has liberated the individual and freed him to make his own choices, to invest, to speculate, to undertake projects, and to maximize his profit—thus adding to the sum total of national production. In letting each individual seek to achieve what he believes to be his own interests, the sum total of production of the nation, and indeed of all nations, will increase. No doubt many projects, many ventures, will fail without harming uninvolved parties, but success of the few will be prodigal.

When the individual is left alone free to choose and struggle, his capacities and potentialities will be unleashed. His inventive and creative capacity will not be stifled or restrained. Moreover, the individual, in his liberty, will be free to join others, to set up a group, a corporation whose members collaborate and cooperate, not only in adding shares to the capital of the corporation, but also in investing their time and insight.

As a result of allowing each person to be completely free, of focusing attention on outcome rather than on a moral private purpose, on the achievements of the corporate body and the efforts and work of specially gifted persons, modern technology has changed the quality of life and transformed the way of living of our age. The amazing achievements of the democratic capitalist society have been acknowledged even by the founders of communism, though they attribute them to the work of a class they call the bourgeoisie, rather than to the spirit of democratic capitalism. This spirit, according to Dr. Novak, fired human intelligence, which was able to open new horizons, and led to the discovery and creation of new goods and to the invention of new methods and new technology.

The main features of democratic capitalism that can be discerned from the work of Dr. Novak are:

- Democratic capitalism consists of three basic elements: a democratic political system, a free economic system, and a moral-cultural system. Without any of these three components, democratic capitalism would perish.
- Each of the three systems that make up the elements of democratic capitalism should respect the autonomy of the two other systems. In exceptional circumstances a system may come to support another system, but it may not control the other system. So, the three component systems of democratic capitalism are not only mutually autonomous but converge and are interdependent.

28

- Just as the province of each of the three systems is separate from that of the other, the powers vested in the political system and distributed among the three branches of government—the legislative, the executive, and the judicial branches—should also be separated and clearly defined with a mechanism of checks and balances.
- Unrestrained liberty of the individual is an inherent feature of democratic capitalism. Thus the individual may seek his own best interests in any way he may choose, letting the invisible hand of God work for the best interest of the nation and of all nations.
- Democratic capitalism is pluralistic, embracing within it all faiths, cultures, and traditions. A tripartite system—political, economic, and moral-cultural—it insists on the separation of powers and is opposed to tyranny, to too much government, and to undue meddling by any of its three components in the affairs of the other two. Its concept of individualism is not a radical one, but is harnessed individualism, which, in a democratic society, is consistent with the concept of communalism. A democratic capitalist is a loyal citizen, a devoted husband, a faithful child, and a responsible father. He is a sympathetic neighbor and a charitable person.
- Emphasis of democratic capitalism on the value of time as a commodity to be invested, has modified the concept of money, which is no longer a static commodity. Wealth is money invested in time, using practical insights. A democratic capitalist saves and endeavors to gain a surplus for further expansion, restlessly looking for new openings, new opportunities, and new ideas.
- An inherent feature of democratic capitalism is the recognition of the right of each person to earn and to own the fruits of his labor. The state and its agencies have no right to dispossess a person or confiscate his property. Democratic capitalist citizens enjoy a deep sense of security and a feeling of continuity. Yet, as they breathe the air of freedom, they recognize their obligation toward the state and their essential loyalty to their fatherland.
- Realistic and practical, democratic capitalism is neither idealistic nor dreamy. It recognizes the intuitive inclinations of the individual and his shortcomings and therefore does not stifle the people's desires or their natural urges.
- Rather than being concerned with immediate personal motives involved in an individual's economic activities, democratic capitalism is concerned with ultimate outcomes and with the well-being of the widest circle of people. By acknowledging the right of every individual to liberty and equal opportunity, by endorsing the individual's right to possess property and all the fruits of his endeavors, by opposing all sorts of oppression and undue limitations, by embracing all

people of all beliefs, and by seeking to achieve a sustained increase in the amount of production, the system serves the cause of world peace and prosperity for all nations. What democratic capitalism does not entertain are impracticable and unachievable dreams such as complete abolition of poverty from the earth, exact equal income for all, and an entirely classless society.

• Democratic capitalism is a system of a free market and an incentive economy. Economic activity consists simply of transactions between consenting parties which involves buying and selling in a reasoned and lawlike contractual manner. In the absence of free markets, there will be no incentives for initiative and successful industries. The phenomenon of free markets is linked to productivity, efficiency, inventiveness, and prosperity.

• Although democratic capitalism presupposes the existence of a stable legal system, it depends less on law than on the competition of interests.

• Democratic capitalism produces large-scale industries and gives rise to economic institutions such as stock exchanges, banks, and other corporations.

• Democratic capitalism can only flourish in a pluralistic social order dominated by a pluralistic spirit. It must be an order of parallel powers that are not centrally dominated, an order in which power cannot be concentrated in the hands of one person or one group.

• The spirit of democratic capitalism rests on the awareness that capital can generate capital, that economic commodities, in addition to their commonly known uses, might have other hidden potential, which, to be discovered, needs investigation, deep observation, and creative endeavor.

Dr. Novak's book begins with an introduction stating the dramatic achievements of democratic capitalism. He contrasts these with conditions during the last decades of the eighteenth century, particularly at the moment of birth of the first democratic capitalist republic in the United States, which coincided with the publication of Adam Smith's *An Inquiry into the Nature and Causes of the Wealth of Nations*. The author laments the failure of the church to understand the spirit of the new economics, which it condemned as materialistic, secular, and dangerous to religion.

Such criticism could not be leveled against Islam, even though the fortunes of Islam at that time were at a very low ebb. Islam, which is a total way of life and makes no distinction between the secular and the spiritual domains, welcomes all progressive ideas and blesses all beneficial achievements like those Dr. Novak attributes to the spirit of democratic capitalism. At that time, particularly at the end of the eighteenth century, the world of Islam, which had suffered wholesale devastation at the hands of the Mongols and the Crusaders, had, for the preceding three centuries, been laboring under the burden of an expanding process of European colonialization that deliberately suppressed all progressive Muslim forces. Ignorant of the merits of Islam and full of prejudices inherited from the era of the Middle Ages, the colonialists viewed Islam with contempt. They regarded it an inferior Oriental culture unfit for modern times and believed that it would die out. Their mission, they thought, was to accelerate the process of its demise through their own authorities and the collaboration of the church schools that were planted everywhere in the Muslim world.

It is no wonder that Dr. Novak—a man of integrity and wisdom but a product of a culture which still suffers from traces of these prejudices, in spite of a great deal of improvement—unwittingly excludes Islam from his statement: "Judaism and Christianity are distinctive among the world religions because they understand salvation as a vocation in history." One does not wish to challenge or argue about the claims he makes on behalf of these two religions, in which we Muslims believe and which we respect and venerate, but my readers will have realized from the previous discussion how Islam, no less than either of these two religions, lays a great emphasis on the role of man in making progressive changes. We may add here the Qur'ānic injunction: "Verily God does not change a people's condition unless they change themselves [13:11]." Thus, John Locke's vision—which Dr. Novak mentions—that history is no longer regarded as cyclical but as progressive, open, and subject to human liberty, is not an unfamiliar notion to Muslims.

The Ideals of Democratic Capitalism

In a short introduction to part 1, the author says that his purpose is to put into words the underlying moral structure which makes the practice of democratic capitalism work. In another place he says that he intends to "elicit a moral-theological theory from the actual practice of democratic capitalism." To justify the need for such a theory, he laments that "Inattention to theory weakens the life of the spirit and injures the capacity of the young to dream of noble purpose." Yet "in previous generations, taking its spiritual inheritance for granted, democratic capitalism felt no acute need for a theory about itself."

To enlighten his reader, the author defines the term "theology" as "sustained reflection upon God and His dealing with the human race, *logos* and *theos*: systematic inquiry about God." The task of the theologian, according to the author, is threefold: (1) to examine the religious implications of the basic economic issues which exist in all economies of all ages—security, investment, work, money, production, distribution, wealth accumulation, division of labor, etc.; (2) to study and evaluate the various systems of political economy: hunting, food-gathering, grazing, agricultural, commercial, feudal, mercantile, capitalist, and socialist economies; and (3) to study and assess institutions, practices, and problems that may arise in a system such as corporations, multinational corporations, bureaucracies, etc. The author's task here is the study of one system—that is, democratic capitalism and the theological theory on which it rests.

In the first chapter, "What Is Democratic Capitalism?" the author lists the weaknesses of and criticisms leveled against capitalism. Muslims agree with many of these criticisms, so Islam does not tolerate taking advantage of the weak or the exploiting of the low human instincts for profit. Then, contrasting contemporary capitalism with the type that developed in the wake of the industrial revolution in Europe, the author describes capitalism and the spirit behind it as it grew in America during the past two hundred years.

The author emphasizes the notion that capitalism is not merely free enterprise but mainly the perception that economic resources have, beyond their commonly known uses, other hidden potentialities. It is the notion that capital can swell, multiply, and increase without having an adverse effect upon others. It is "the spirit of development, risk, experiment, adventure. It surrenders present security for future betterment." It has made the state and the economy two different things, introducing "a novel pluralism into the very center of the social system."

In moving words Dr. Novak writes the story of his own conversion from a staunch adherent of socialism, or rather democratic socialism, to a strong advocate of democratic capitalism. In the course of the story, Dr. Novak demonstrates the inconsistencies inherent in democratic socialism. He rightly states that the issue of planning was no longer a dividing line in this respect since "To plan ahead is human," but to plan coercively is not democratic. If planning is fashioned by local communities, it is no longer central, and the result will look like democratic capitalist economy.

In defining the term democratic capitalism, the author traces the thoughts and theories of other modern economic philosophers who, before him, struggled to identify the spirit behind democratic capitalism, the force that moved and is moving it. In this regard, he quotes from R. H. Tawney's *Religion and the Rise of Capitalism* the notion that the dominant spiritual theme in democratic capitalism is "the vulgar itch of acquisitiveness." He also discusses at length Max Weber's views, in particular Weber's claim that commerce in a capitalist society acquires "a new meaning" in "a new spirit." Novak also mentions Max Weber's description of the spirit of capitalism as something like "a powerful synthesis of religion and economic striving."

In my own view, the restless itch of acquisitiveness which has always been with man could not by itself have given rise to capitalism at the time of its growth in Western society. Similarly, the encounter between religion and economic striving has occurred since the beginning of Islam, and economic activities are interwoven with the religious thought of preliterate societies everywhere. The notion that work and labor in business or agriculture could lead to an increase in profits and harvests without causing a shortage elsewhere must have existed among early peoples, though it was a simple, not a complex, notion. Moreover, attributing the birth of capitalism to a new turn in religious thinking seems to me to be speculation.

Capitalism in the simple sense of free enterprise, leading to sustained growth, though at a slower rate, existed centuries before the advent of the modern large-scale type of Western capitalism. The emergence of this modern, more spectacular pattern of capitalism, which was a departure from religion, was, I feel, the result of a combination of factors which took place in Western society: the release of stifled souls from the shackles of the feudal system during the Middle Ages; the emergence of a spirit of adventure among the colonizers; the tremendous potential of the vast resources of raw materials discovered in the occupied territories; and last but not least the invention of machinery which made possible the growth of heavy industries and the development of large factories. I also believe that the break with the old domestic ties, which caused a deep feeling of the need to substitute the individual's personal efforts and initiative for the old ethnic ties to provide a sense of security, must have inspired an inventive spirit that looked for new horizons for success.

I share Dr. Novak's admiration for John Locke's observation that "Nature is far wealthier in possibilities than human beings had ever drawn attention to before," not only quantitatively, in the sense of abundance, but also in hidden potentialities. Yet, I am not comfortable with the author's remark that, "humans are called upon to be co-creators with God," which paraphrases Locke's statement. Islam's pure concept of monotheism rejects any notion of a co-creator or partnership with God, Who is Perfect, One, and Unique in every respect. We could say instead that human beings are called upon to unravel the secrets of nature and should endeavor to discover the potentialities hidden in God's creations. The Holy Qur'ān is not only

33

full of references to the abundance of bounties in the earth but also invites people to use their wisdom to discover the secrets of nature and put them to good use. In these words, the Holy Book explains the wisdom of making the abundant benefits of the natural resources accessible only through reflection, investigation, research, and hard work: "And if God were to enlarge the provision for His servants they would surely have transgressed beyond all bounds in the earth, but He sends (it) down by measures as He wills [42:27]." Perhaps Dr. Novak's analysis is the best commentary on this verse: "If there were total abundance, immediately accessible to all, economic activity would be pointless. But under conditions of scarcity, human beings need each other. Scarcity calls economic activism into existence. . . . This fact alone diminishes anarchy."

I admire the author's commentary on Max Weber's six points of capitalism: freedom of labor; reasoning, self-criticism, and self-improvement; sustained enterprising; differentiation between the household and the workplace; a stable network of law and organization; and urbanism. That is, Dr. Novak makes the observation that Weber failed to analyze the relationship "between economic liberty and political liberty." They are two different concepts (democracy and capitalism), neither can exist without the other. Weber failed to view the new system as democratic capitalism, rather than mere capitalism. Far from being an "iron cage," as Weber described it, democratic capitalism is open, dynamic, innovative, self-correcting, and inventive. It honors hard work, labor, and commerce, and no longer regards menial work as a mean pursuit. Its founders "championed the vision of one world and sustained economic development for the entire world." This vision is quite Islamic, except that the point of departure here is individual liberty and satisfaction and happiness on earth. In Islam the compelling motive is the desire to please God through hard work and service to oneself and others in obedience to the divine command. Happiness on earth, to a Muslim, is satisfaction in conforming with God's will through obedience to the Qur'ānic guidance. It is a by-product of the effort to seek happiness in the hereafter with God.

The author's remark that Islamic and Oriental cultures "had long mercantile traditions . . . and traditions of science and technique . . . but never produced the link in spirit required for the 'take off' of modernity" reveals a little lack of information about the reality of this strong link in Islam. The industrial-commercial, scientific, and technological progress of Muslims in the Middle Ages, which the author acknowledges, was severely checked and blocked by the terror and savage devastation of the Mongol and Tatar wars, which destroyed

34

whole cities and demolished all the renowned centers of Islamic learning, eliminating almost all the inhabitants, including the scholars, burning libraries, and eradicating almost all sources of enlightenment. Decades, even centuries of terror, destruction, wholesale murder, and barbaric torture at the hands of the Crusaders and the Mongols brought stagnation, retardation, and ignorance. For centuries, the aim of those who survived—dislocated, impoverished, and superstitious—was to cling to life and to their faith and to transmit the basic framework of their religion and its Holy Scripture to their posterity. The long age of European colonization, which took advantage of this vacuum, did very little to improve the situation.

Among the modern writers whom Dr. Novak appears to admire most is Maritain, a French author and diplomat who was quite fascinated by the pattern of capitalism in America. Maritain almost grasped the moral-cultural spirit behind capitalism. Dr. Novak then criticizes the silence of the Christian authorities on this moral element and concludes by saying, "My aim is to break that silence."

The author, in the next chapter, regards pluralism as the main feature of democratic capitalism. The democratic capitalist society is basically a pluralistic social order that is contrary to the concept of unitary order. Yet, pluralism is not disorder. It is meant to safeguard against the accumulation of too much power. In the author's words, "a pluralistic society has a conception of a social order radically different from the unitary order of traditionalistic and socialistic societies."

Of course the author has in mind the European traditionalistic society. The Muslim traditional social order is unitary in one sense and pluralistic in another. It is unitary in the sense that it seeks to organize itself on the basis of one moral scheme of guidance, as revealed by God through His Messengers. This guidance should protect against a unitary power and against absolutism and should permit, and indeed encourage, a pluralistic social order in the way Dr. Novak describes.

The Islamic social order is not empty at the center. The center's seat is to be occupied by a responsible authority elected by the *ummah*, the community, to see to it that the revealed guidance, believed to be in the best interest of the community, is duly applied and respected.

The social order, as Dr. Novak emphasizes, should permit individual variation and doubts, and requires the separation of systems, the distribution of powers, and the establishment of institutions that watch each other but cooperate with one another. So the political system, while refraining from interfering in the individual's liberty and choices and from controlling the economic and moral-cultural systems, has to play certain economic roles that cannot be undertaken by tycoons. It has to protect the soundness of the currency and formulate favorable terms for international trade and regulate internal competition. The moral-cultural system, for its part, may not unduly meddle in the affairs of the economy, but it plays an indispensable role in inculcating self-discipline, encouraging hard work, inspiring integrity, sacrifice, companionship, and generosity. Moreover, the economic worker—a farmer, an industrialist, or a businessman—is a responsible citizen who seeks the truth and is committed to the political success of his country.

In discussing pluralism, Dr. Novak makes some admirable observations:

> The [major] aim of democratic capitalism is to establish the practical substructure of cooperative social life. . . . Without bringing their metaphysical, philosophical or religious presuppositions into dispute, diverse persons can agree to cooperate in specific activities, to sign contracts specifying limited mutual responsibilities, and in other ways work together without imposing their moral views or ultimate visions of life upon each other. . . . To enter such a [pluralistic] society, one need not surrender one's native culture, religion, conception of life, scheme of values, way of philosophizing, personal vision. No statement of unitary belonging is required, no denunciation of world-views previously held. One must pledge only to respect the practical principles set forth in [its] constitution.

To the extent that the principle of pluralism ensures the liberty of various segments of the society as well as that of individuals, and allows diversity and variation within the permissible scheme of morality, it is quite excellent. One wishes that the so-called third-world societies would learn from this marvelous experience of the West and try to reform themselves in the light of this experience. Although it offers no new teaching to Islam, it provides an excellent and workable framework for Islam's teaching of equality, liberty, equal opportunity, and the ideal of working to achieve success on earth.

Yet, as indicated earlier, the doctrine of pluralism should not be so exaggerated as to deny a central moral order suffusing all systems in society. I, as a Muslim, therefore, do not subscribe to the author's warning that "grave dangers to the human spirit lurk in the subordination of the political system or the economic system to a single moral-cultural vision." We should be careful, however, when we use the term "culture" and its derivatives. It is better to use the term "moral" alone. Culture is a human feature, developed by a people

36

through their historical experience. It varies from one people to another and also from one time to another. Moral principles are distinguished by their perpetuity and their inherent values. Yet, Dr. Novak often lumps them together as if culture and morality are at the same level. We might therefore agree with his statement, "When moral and cultural visions of certain sorts prevail, a democratic policy and a capitalist economy are not feasible," if he deletes the word "moral." He too concedes that "there is an inner consonance between the inherent respect for free acts of faith and conscience common to Judaism and Christianity [and Islam], and the rights protected by democracy."

I reiterate that no danger is likely to arise from subordinating the political and the economic systems to a sensible, progressive moral order which takes into account all human needs, especially when this order is designed and revealed by the Lord, the Creator who knows what is best for human beings at all times. We can call the political economic system based on this moral order capitalism or any other name. The main point is that the system should provide and respect the merits which Dr. Novak claims for democratic capitalism and which are certainly included within the framework of Islam—namely, the legitimacy of private ownership, the freedom of private enterprise, a free market economy with effective incentives, and so forth. In a truly Muslim order, there would be no fear of dominance by a class of clergymen who would control the economic life, bestowing licenses, imposing taxes or tariffs, as churchmen did in the past, because Islam does not embrace the idea of a religious class of people. In Islam all people are equal and have immediate access to God. Only men of knowledge are especially honored,[2] and knowledge is available for all to learn. Moreover, the basis of the pluralistic scheme was laid down by the Prophet Muhammad himself when he told his Companions: "You know better all matters pertaining to your worldly life." The pluralistic order is certainly healthy, but will be more perfect when it is enlightened by the moral guidance of God, which will inspire a sense of unity, warmth, and dependence on the Almighty, the Creator. As such there will be no large-scale suffering from a sense of loss, alienation, anomie, loneliness, nothingness, or a denial of the higher and subtler human characteristics and requirements. As Dr. Novak admits in a later chapter, "Precisely because rational self-interest does not always result in a moral outcome, religious [and other] values are indispensable to democratic capitalism."

It is true that human beings behave as though they are unavoidably enmeshed in lies, betrayals, injustice, and sinful activities, but it would be a gloomy and unfair view of humanity to generalize and characterize all humanity this way. There is always pressure by the satanic forces to do evil, to cheat, steal, lie, and so on, but it is an exaggeration to assert that the evil forces can more often conquer a human conscience nourished by religious upbringing and constantly inspired by the light of the Scriptures and the prayers to our Creator and Nourisher. It may be true that there is no perfect Christian society, or perfect Jewish society, or perfect Muslim society. Nevertheless, one cannot understand why a political economic society based on the divine moral guidance should end in disaster. Such a system would aspire to approach the ideal, not necessarily to achieve it in full. We Muslims therefore do not endorse Dr. Novak's reluctance to Christianize the economic system. Revealed religion in its pure form does not restrain liberty or forbid diversity of opinion outside the basic framework of beliefs. It encourages taking into account the interests and views of all segments of society. As Dr. Novak rightly states, agreement of the majority will not be far from the mark. The Prophet Muhammad said, "My nation will never agree on an error."[3]

In his eloquent discussion of the concept of emergent probability, the author emphasizes the role played by Adam Smith in grasping this notion and credits him with calling for a new order in which each individual is left free to use his insight, to explore emergent probabilities, taking into account the vision of failure yet spurred by probable success. More often failure occurs but at no cost to society. When success happens, it will be for the benefit of all. Dr. Novak, therefore, reiterates the necessity of guarding against political control of the economic system except when intervention is needed, for example, to regulate commercial competition and protect the currency.

To a person of Islamic background—whose faith erased all class differences fourteen hundred years ago, restored all basic human rights, stressed the merits of hard work by hand or by brain, and commanded the faithful to exploit nature's potential—the lavish praise heaped on one who grasped the need to free the individual to realize his capabilities stirs greater admiration for his own religion.

Dr. Novak then discusses the concept of sin and gives a summary of its theological implications. He is at his best in defending the pursuit of personal "best interests" as a morally virtuous motive. Muslims agree with, and see no evil implication in, this pursuit so long as it does not lead to injustice toward others and is not so exaggerated as to become greed. Self-interest not merely is individualistic but also includes the interests of those about whom the individual is concerned, such as the members of his family, his neighbors, and his community. We do not expect all people, or even many people, to be altruistic. In pursuing self-interest, which is certainly the greatest stimulus for productive work, we expect the achievement of the common good in the best interest of everybody. This pursuit is not, in the Muslim view, a sin. It is just like seeking to fulfill sexual desire within the bond of marriage. We do enjoy it sensually, but it is not by any means a sin.

This does not mean that we, as theologians, should explicitly and openly declare indifference to sin as such—that is, the violation of the command of God—even when the temporal law condones it. Dr. Novak seems to be too tolerant when he says that the political economy "is designed for sinners" or that human institutions "will always be marked by sin." Muslims do not regard this sort of license to be a necessary ingredient for the success of a democratic economy, nor do we see in the call for self-control and upholding moral virtues any undue restraint on the liberty of economic action. Nor do we violate the privacy of a person when we object to instances of public violations of moral decency. Moreover, we do not see a conflict between our concern over the immediate personal motive behind an economic action and a healthy ultimate outcome for society. The better the immediate motive, the greater and healthier the outcome. Personal purpose and ultimate outcome can be harmonized so as to conform with divine purpose and human best interests.

God has granted us freedom and the ability to choose between sin and virtue, not to become habitual sinners and open violators of His commands. Why does democratic capitalism have to "represent the hearts of human beings, not as they should be, but as they are," as Dr. Novak argues? As theologians and men of religion, shouldn't we be concerned with human behavior as it should be? Or are we to surrender to empirical realities and condone indecency including trading in human flesh, in pornographic material, and the business of massage parlors? Muhammad, the Prophet of Islam, warned: "Every piece of human flesh nourished by consumption [of food the price of which is] of doubtful source, will burn in the Hellfire."[4] To be in harmony with Islam, democratic capitalism needs to be purified and freed from such moral license. Dr. Novak's next words, however, have a healing effect, and one cannot agree more with his optimism: "Simple reflection . . . suggests that there are enormous reservoirs of high motivation and moral purpose among citizens in democratic capitalism."

These words stir fond memories in the writer's mind, memories of wonderful experiences of kindness and sympathy extended to my family and myself during our stay in the West, especially in England when I started my studies there in the early 1950s. One could relate many beautiful stories about the sympathetic treatment extended to us by our British neighbors, by the registrar and professors at my school in London, and my helpful professor at the University of Cambridge. Perhaps unbridled liberty, as much as it unleashes human potential for large-scale economic success, inspires deeper self-respect reflected in greater trust, sympathy, and respect for fellow human beings. It is paradoxical, however, that a society of such a high order of morality should be a fertile ground for cruel street muggings and widespread networks of organized crime. Nevertheless, the author talks of transforming the sinful energy into creative use, and agreeably remarks in conclusion that democratic capitalism has attempted to draw from self-interest its most creative potential.

In the chapter on providence and practical wisdom, Dr. Novak demonstrates how time and practical intelligence have their economic value. By using money in time with practical wisdom, money grows and increases, without any adverse effect upon the wealth of others. Thus time has great value and should always be wisely invested. Practical wisdom also makes democratic capitalism a spiritual concept. So in the author's view, democratic capitalism is not entirely a materialistic vision. Wealth, as a result, is not simply the tangible idle money; it is money invested by intelligence in time. Money has become intellectualized, to some extent, as a psychological reality.

Here too Dr. Novak correctly defends the merits of the institution of the free market, in which countless transactions are better predicted by millions of free economic agents. Economic behavior, which cannot be anarchical and has its proper discipline and laws, cannot occur in isolation. It means people coming together in a reasoned, lawlike, contractual way. Without free markets, there would be fewer incentives for inventiveness and hard work. It is true, as the author asserts, that a defense of the free market is a defense of efficiency, productivity, inventiveness, and prosperity. It is also true that it is a defense of the free conscience in the realm of the spirit, politics, and the economic decisions of everyday life; and a defense of the pluralistic order against the unitary and commanded order of socialism. Dr. Novak's interpretation of Adam Smith's phrase "the invisible hand," in the sense of a mysterious guidance, is magnificent. When everyone tries to achieve his own interests independently and separately, common good is achieved as if a deliberate intelligent concealed force has been at work, coordinating activities toward a common desired end. The author's defense of the merits of trade and of making a reasonable profit deserves our wholehearted support. As was explained earlier, Islam honors the pursuit of economic goals in the form of trade or manual work. As we will also recall, the Prophet Muhammad promoted a free market and condemned the imposition of tolls and hoarding.

Dr. Novak's eloquent comment on the value of time as an economic commodity, which developed as part of the total concept of democratic capitalism within the past two hundred years, fills me, a Muslim, with a new appreciation of the progressive guidance of Islam. No religious tradition emphasizes the value of time more than the Islamic religion, not only as an economic commodity but also as a precious entity to be expended in legitimate activity. One of the best activities the individual may engage in is to make peace between disputing parties. Other agreeable activities include using time to reflect on and ponder the mysteries of God's creations and to learn some useful knowledge. Another worthy way of spending time is to use it in seeking one's living. We are forbidden to waste time, and all ritual duties are associated with time.

The Prophet said: "The feet of the son of Adam will not cross the Bridge [over Hellfire leading to Paradise] until he has [satisfactorily] answered these questions: how he expended his life time; how he used his youthful energy; and how he earned his wealth and how he spent it."[5] The Prophet also said: "Take from your youthful time for the time of your old age; from the time of your wealth to the time of your poverty; and from the time of your earthly life to life after death."[6]

Each of the five daily prayers of Islam has a prescribed period within which it has to be performed. It cannot be performed ahead of time, nor can it be deferred to a later time. The zakat also has its own dates. Fasting takes place at certain prescribed hours, and the pilgrimage to Mecca has its own season. According to a famous tradition "Time is like a sword [threatening you]; unless you break it, it will cut you."[7]

In his chapter on community, the author is at pains to stress the absence of conflict between the concept of individualism and the notion of communalism, both of which are characteristics of democratic capitalism. Here it is not a vicious or capricious individualism but an individualism responsible to the welfare of the community, to the state, the moral order, and fellow human beings. It is individualism of liberty within the law and within the framework of this responsibility. Nonetheless, democratic capitalism is communal. Its aim is to increase production and the total wealth of all nations. It is built on cooperation and produces communal institutions such as stock exchanges, banks, corporate bodies, and national and multinational corporations.

41

Dr. Novak points out four elements in the structure of democratic capitalism: (1) concern for *world development* (the wealth of nations), (2) *the corporation*, (3) *interdependence*, and (4) the ethos of *cooperation*. Democratic capitalists, he says, have a sense of a shared ethos. Toward the end of the chapter, he makes this encouraging statement: "The ideal of a democratic capitalist society is to guarantee the right of each person to pursue happiness. . . . Since it is in the nature of humans to be social, the ideal is also to build decent and even affectionate relations among those who work together."

In the chapter on the communitarian individual, Dr. Novak rejects the accusation made by the enemies of democratic capitalism who condemn it as a bourgeois system of despised individualism. He also laments the misunderstanding that Anglo-Saxon culture is individualistic and defends it on the grounds that in practice the customs and traditions of that culture nourish remarkable social orderliness and a cooperative spirit. He then proceeds to exonerate the system of capitalism in light of the writing of Adam Smith. The author then discusses the "assault on the bourgeoisie."

The very idea of classes—of aristocrats, the bourgeoisie, and the proletariat—is not a Muslim concept. Equality is basic in Islam, both as a belief and as a practice. Ideas and doctrines belong to all segments of society. No one layer of society may arrogate to itself exclusively such doctrines. Nor is it right to condemn any particular class as such. It is all right to condemn the evils of wealth, for example, but not a class or a race.

In the chapter on the family, which is a strong mediating structure, Dr. Novak demonstrates, in admirable terms, how this fundamental institution, in its traditional "nostalgic" form, released from feudal restrictions and prejudices, has been a training ground in liberty, self-sacrifice, and adventurism. The family is the institution that preserves and inculcates 3,000 years of human heritage; the family is where the human infant is morally and physically trained. The notion of sexual liberation is rightly rejected by the author, who also condemns irresponsible efforts to break up the family.

Dr. Novak explains how family obligations serve as a prompting factor for economic growth and thrift, how concern over the needs of one's offsprings compels hard work. Even political discipline and the virtue of self-control are learned at home. Spouses are also mirrors for one another. The conjugal relationship, being so intimate, open and frank, and long lasting, reaches deeply below the surface and reveals otherwise hidden realities.

In this regard, much of Dr. Novak's writing about the significance of the family agrees with the ideas and ideals of Islam, except that Islam looks at the family as a wider circle. Dr. Novak's concern, it seems, is related to the nuclear family, one's immediate relatives, the modern industrial family. This is indeed the core of the family in Islam. Yet, some obligations are also owed to other relatives, even when they are far from the center. Mutual rights and obligations are concentrated at the center—that is, among parents, children, grandchildren, and siblings—and involve the rights of maintenance and inheritance. Such rights and obligations, to a lesser degree, are extended to other blood relatives and are real and significant, even if a relative belongs to a different religion. These obligations are not merely secular or legal, but are also within the scope of fulfilling one's religious obligations, thereby pleasing God and earning His reward. As such, loyalty to the Creator and to the community of the faithful, which is the first priority, is harmonized with the individual's ethnic loyalty. The individual remains a part of his blood group, but does not dissolve within it. Family obligations should not stand in the way of one's obligations to the Creator, nor does one lose one's individuality.

In the chapter on "continuous revolution," Dr. Novak further analyzes the three component systems of democratic capitalism. He quotes Daniel Bell's *Cultural Contradictions of Capitalism* concerning the "three distinct realms [of contemporary society] each of which is obedient to a different axial principle": equality for the polity, efficiency for economics, and self-fulfillment for the moral-cultural component. Dr. Novak then adds more axial principles for each: liberty and solvency and monetary and trade policy for politics, attentiveness to human needs for economics, and ethics and moral values for the moral-cultural system. Moreover, a political system is greater than a state because the former includes political parties, public opinion, lobbies, and the ballot box. The differentiation and separation of powers into executive, judicial and legislative branches, should guard against tyranny.

The author concludes the chapter by warning that "A war of ideas is being fought in many minds and hearts. Many, battling in this war, change their minds. Within us, there is a battle between the competing ideals of democratic capitalism and democratic socialism. On its outcome, the future shape of our society depends." The author, unfortunately, seems indifferent to another option, the success of which is likely to affect, in some degree, the future shape of all societies. This is the aspiration of millions of people scattered all over the globe to see Islam and its ideals, which are now encountering Western ideologies, restored in all spheres of life in the world of Islam.

The Twilight of Socialism

In the second part of his book, Dr. Novak reiterates the basic theses and most of the views elucidated in part 1. Therefore, my review here and of the next part of the book will be shorter and less detailed.

A reader of the second part easily gets the impression that the author's aim is to show the merits of democratic capitalism over other systems, particularly Marxism and socialism which he continues to criticize, revealing their impracticability and the harsh tyranny and sufferings that led to everywhere they were attempted.

After celebrating the demise of socialism in a short introduction, the author discusses in a separate chapter what he calls the transformation of socialism into a form of liberalism that permits a limited degree of liberty denied under the Marxist system.

In the chapter on socialism as highmindedness, Dr. Novak makes an eloquent moral comparison between democratic socialism of which he was an adherent earlier, and democratic capitalism, to which he later converted. Disillusioned with socialism's unrealistic dreams and unworkable ideals, Novak explains that it was this unreality that was wrong with socialism. He says that an unworkable ideal is no real ideal and that democratic socialism has "narrowing impact upon social life." He then explains how socialism is inconsistent with the concept of democracy, and how democratic socialism has dissolved into a moral vision. He quotes approvingly a Romanian dissident who wrote: "Socialism . . . has not given a valuable solution to mankind and always comes into conflict with freedom, democracy, and justice."

Dr. Novak concludes the chapter with an interesting section on the value of having a small, very rich segment in society. There is an aesthetic, recreational, and generally cultural value in having in the society such a very wealthy minority (about 1 percent of the population in the United States who earn more than $100,000 annually), with their special tastes, their elegance and eccentricities. Dr. Novak favors the reality of unequal income and unequal achievements, a natural feature of human life reflected and explained as well in the Qur'ān.[8]

In the chapter on the distribution of income, and the problems of black Americans, the author argues against a ceiling on the amount of income a citizen may earn. He sympathetically treats the problems of black Americans and urges members of the black community to assume an attitude of greater initiative and to seize opportunities through personal initiative.

The final chapter of part 2 is devoted to a discussion of the phenomenon of multinational (transnational) corporations, their advantages to host countries, and the opportunities they present for better international relations. Corporations, he said, are built on bonds of trust, good faith, and mutual desire for greater achievements. Ironically, "a system which encourages all to seek first their own interests yields liberty and receives in return loyalty and love. . . . The economic system of democratic capitalism is more universal than its political or moral-cultural systems," and therefore "business firms are easier for nations around the world to import than are political parties, churches or religion."

We Muslims share Dr. Novak's criticism of socialism and Marxism for two reasons. One is our hesitation to share their unrealistic and unachievable objective—namely, to set up a universal classless social order that transcends national and racial loyalties and in which man will become a new being motivated only by the principle of human solidarity, comradeliness, and communal interest. In such an order, they dream, there will be no poverty or inequality of income, but each will give according to his ability and will take according to his needs. Socialism has failed badly to achieve this objective. There has been no improvement in the distribution of income, nor has there been any real equality or true brotherhood of the type they describe. National and ethnic loyalties have proved to be more powerful than dogmatic loyalty to socialism.

We also condemn socialism for its tyrannical program and the harsh measures it unjustly uses forcibly to impose its impractical aim. These unjust measures include the confiscation of property and placing the ownership of all economic resources with the state, which under this system, in the Soviet sphere, controls the entire national economy. Thus decision making and power are concentrated in the hands of politicians and government officials who may be corrupt and inefficient. They strangle the citizens' freedom and kill the individual's initiative. Life without liberty is lifeless. Central-government planning of the economy and the abolition of private ownership rob the individual of the incentive to take the initiative and to work hard. They deny him his birthright—the liberty to work, to choose, to earn, and to own the fruits of his labor.

"Equality" is an attractive word. It is the birthright of every human being, but what does it mean? It means equality in the sight of God; only good deeds and righteousness count in His eyes. It means the right of every person to be treated with dignity, to live, to learn, to own property, and to have equal opportunity. In this sense, equality is emphatically endorsed by Islam. What it does not mean is equality

45

with respect to material fortune, a condition that socialists have un-successfully tried to impose. We are all created with different degrees of intelligence, ability, and talents and with different inclinations and potential. We also possess a nature that can be stimulated, through incentives and rewards, to work hard. No power, no political system, can transform or modify human nature. Divine wisdom has deter-mined that we are to be of different attainments, and the resulting mosaic makes life more interesting. According to the Qur'ān, the expectation of higher achievement is in itself a powerful factor:

> And God has favored some of you above others in provision. Now those who are more favored will by no means hand over their provision to those whom their right hands pos-sess, so that they may be equal with them in respect thereof [16:71].

> We have apportioned among them their livelihood in the life of this world, and raised some of them above others in rank that some of them may take labor from others; and the mercy of your Lord is better than [the wealth] which they amass [43:32].

So differences in the attainment of worldly success is the divine wisdom, but material success should not carry with it any superior moral value. Only righteousness counts. A free economy promotes prosperity, creativity, inventiveness, and satisfaction. Socialism, whenever it has been imposed, has led to tyranny, injustice, wide-scale oppression, shortage, long queues, fear, and misery.

I recall my own experience when, after a three-day stay in West Berlin in the early 1960s, I went to the other side for a few hours' visit in the company of a student guide from Frei University. As soon as we passed through the dividing wall, my companion looked seized with apprehension. "Are you scared?" I asked. "Yes!" was the an-swer. What a contrast! From bustling ease and open prosperity be-hind us, we moved into a gray, silent climate. The few people we met in the street looked pale and tense. Shop windows looked dull, their poor displays reflecting scarcity and less refinement. The East Ger-man professor at the university who began our interview in his office with a lecture on the merits of socialism, suddenly lowered his voice and whispered to me about the oppression the people there were suffering. As soon as we crossed the wall back in to West Berlin in the evening, we breathed a deep sigh of relief.

What is actually needed are measures to narrow the gap arising from inequality in financial status and to ameliorate the miseries of poverty. In a democratic capitalist society, this is accomplished, as

Dr. Novak says, through taxation, welfare legislation, and government regulation of trade and industry. In Islam, this is done in two ways. First, the emphasis is laid on the merits of work and the condemnation of looking for charity. Another method includes the institution of the zakat, which as we have already mentioned is the obligation of charities, giving to the needy, maintaining the duty to pay the cost of living of certain relatives, the mechanism of inheritance, and the right of the state to collect special taxes when needed.

These measures have worked successfully and effectively, and, as was mentioned earlier, at certain times in the history of Islam, no poor persons could be found to receive the zakat. The abolition of private ownership, the monopoly of the state over all economic resources, the use of cruel measures, and usurping people's liberty are not effective solutions to the inequitable distribution of wealth. The greatest merit of democratic capitalism, in my view, is its commitment to human liberty, though it pays little attention to the motives accompanying human activity and concentrates instead on the ultimate outcome. Another weakness is its indifference to the moral legitimacy of the type of economic action, a feature that has led to undesirable results in democratic capitalist society. A democratic capitalist does not hesitate to open a gambling casino, a liquor store, or a porno shop. Out of sight of the law enforcement agencies, he would not hesitate to do anything that would increase his wealth, including distribution of forbidden drugs. Islam, no less than democratic capitalism, protects and defends the individual's right to liberty—not only his economic freedom but also his freedom to choose his faith, the most fundamental issue in any religion. The Holy Qur'ān declares: "So let them who wish to embrace the truth do so, and let those who wish to reject the truth do so [18:29]." "There shall be no compulsion in the matter of religion [2:256]."

Nonetheless, free human action, unlike instinctive action in animals, has to be guided by wisdom and limited by a respect for the liberty and rights due to other people. It must also be guided by the wisdom of the divine teachings. Human liberty therefore operates within a wide area, bounded only by these considerations. Stepping outside the bounds brings it into collision with the rights of others and harms the community. If an action when universalized could threaten the survival of the community, then that action must be forbidden and it is no longer within the domain of human liberty. If everyone made his living through gambling, robbery, pornography, or practicing usury, then the community would die out. It is only such harmful pursuits that are forbidden in Islam.

We certainly agree with Dr. Novak's wisdom in arguing against the idea of imposing a limit on the amount of money a person can earn within a year. In truth, it is better for the economy to have a small percentage of the very wealthy. It is indeed better for culture, art, and literature. This position is in agreement with Islam, which imposes no limit as to the income of a person, on two conditions: income must be earned through lawful means, and all dues, such as the zakat and other obligations, must be paid.

A Theology of Economics

In his concern with the theological-moral content of democratic capitalism and with its integrity, Dr. Novak looks first at the ideals and the theological-moral elements and presuppositions of democratic capitalism and calls for laying the foundation of a new discipline of a theology of economics. He laments the fact that while there is plenty of literature on the theology of socialism, "there is virtually nothing on the theology of democratic capitalism." He urges theologians to be concerned with the study of three orders: (1) economic concepts such as work, money, scarcity, production, distribution, capital, wages, and labor; (2) various political economic systems, such as capitalism, socialism, feudalism, and the mercantile systems; and (3) particular institutions within systems, such as banks and corporations.

The author then proceeds to clarify his favorite political economic philosophy, which crystallizes in democratic capitalism, by criticizing its enemies. In the chapter on the Catholic anti-capitalist tradition, Dr. Novak reviews the statements made against democratic capitalism by Catholic church leaders, especially the popes. The underlying theme of these criticisms is the accusation that democratic capitalism is individualistic, selfish, and materialistic and leads to inequality. Although the author does not categorically refute the criticisms, he simply says, after reflecting on the question of development, "One would think that Catholic theologians in particular, would be more modest in speaking of development. The record of wholly Catholic countries in the history of economics and social development is not entirely laudable. The same is true also of their record in establishing democracy."

In studying, analyzing, and criticizing Christian socialism in Europe, Dr. Novak selects the case of Juergen Moltmann, an outstanding European theologian who has had a great deal of influence on Latin American liberation theology. In his work *The Theology of*

Hope, Moltmann focuses attention on the future of man and emphasizes the eschatological aspects of Christian thinking and the social and political nature of the Christian vocation. According to Novak, Moltmann's "intention seems to be to articulate a new 'Protestant ethic' that would bring Christianity to the support of socialism." Moltmann advocates some sort of "moral idealism," which he calls "social democracy" or "democratic socialism." Moltmann "has tried to change the Protestant understanding of God and of human history under the cross and resurrection of Jesus Christ." The former understanding "for him, reveals the ambiguity of history which identifies Christianity with the poor and the oppressed, the latter he employs as grounds of a theology of hope." He "posits two parties whose dialogue gives most promise for the future, 'humanistic Marxism aligned with the downtrodden and the humiliated' and humanistic Christianity which is chiliastic, future-oriented, and concerned for the poor," but he does not conceive of "a marriage between humanistic Christianity and humanistic capitalism." Dr. Novak criticizes Moltmann because of the latter's "tendency to subordinate the economic system to the political system," and his failure "to glimpse the humanistic interactions of democratic capitalism." He "imagines capitalism as though it were a kind of prostitution: outside the law, destructive of true community, reducing all relations to impersonal monetary relations, inspiring wolflike animosity between man and man, mad and irrational in its pursuit of growth for the sake of growth and work for the sake of work." Dr. Novak then traces Moltmann's criticism, point by point, exploring his errors. He refutes, for example, Moltmann's criticism that "economic categories are more comprehensible than political ones, and political institutions are less and less able to regulate the large-scale economic organization." Dr. Novak rejects this criticism on the grounds that, first, "economic activities are more rational and community building than politics," and second, Moltmann is not aware of the power and extent of government regulations in a democratic capitalist society. Dr. Novak also criticizes Moltmann because "he offers no reason why government officials should be more trusted with economic decisions, when free individuals may not be so," because he "respects political liberties and moral-cultural liberties, but not economic liberties," and because "his theology of economics gives very little place for economics," subordinating "economics to a system of political allocation and moral-theological dominance."

In the chapter "Guilt for Third World Poverty," Dr. Novak defends the democratic capitalist nations, or the developed countries, against the accusation that they are the cause of the poverty of the so-called third-world nations, that the developed countries impose unfavorable terms in international trade, create privileged centers to exploit the periphery, promote unworkable or clumsy projects, and act illegally through multinational corporations. Reflecting on the accusations, he says evidence does not seem to support them.

The author then examines the theology of liberation, developed within the Catholic church in Latin America, which rendered valuable "services to the sick and the infirm, the insane and the orphaned and those in need of education, and counseling, and other forms of humanitarian assistance." Yet, the "vocations of commerce and industry, entrepreneurship and economic activism, were treated with the distancing traditional to Catholicism in aristocratic societies." "Economic activism was suspect as 'materialism,' " and "is not given high spiritual value." Liberation theology tends to be integral, unitary, holistic, and otherworldly, concentrating on the poor rather than on production and failing to see worldly life as a spiritual vocation. Quoting Michael Dodson, Dr. Novak criticizes liberation theologians because instead of learning from the gospel "and then applying their insights to the actual world," the liberation theologians "try to learn from the world and then 'locate' their experience in the gospel."

Discussing a theology of development with special reference to Latin America, Dr. Novak rejects Archbishop Dom Helder Camara's Brazilian lament before the World Council of Churches in 1970, "that 80 percent of the world's resources are at the disposal of 20 percent of the world's inhabitants." This is "not exactly true," Dr. Novak says, citing the fact that most of the world's oil, for example, is in the hands of third-world nations. Dr. Novak blames Latin American countries and the Catholic aristocratic ethic for their economic retardation, since they emphasize luck, chauvinism, and status figures, rather than a truly productive ethic, "which values diligent work, steadfast regularity, and the responsible seizure of opportunity."

Dr. Novak rejects the claim that the growing wealth of the industrial nations caused the poverty of the other nations. He says that this claim is based on the assumption of a static, total sum of economic resources, which means that when wealth grows somewhere, it is diminished or disappears somewhere else. Yet, capital has been proved to be capable of growth in itself without adverse effect on the wealth of others. Also, according to Dr. Novak, 80 percent, or even 90 percent, of the world's economic resources were discovered and put to good use through invention and creativity. The author observes that liberation theologians seem to favor socialism when they write about institutions, but seem to favor economic independence, self-reliance, personal creativity, and self-determination when they write about individuals. It remains to be seen whether the church in Latin America will "encourage its people along the road to unitary socialism—or along the road of pluralistic democratic capitalism."

In the chapter "From Marxism to Democratic Capitalism," Dr. Novak relates the story of Reinhold Niebuhr, a notable American thinker. Niebuhr became an eloquent advocate of socialism early in the 1930s and then moved slowly and steadily over the next three decades to embrace the tenets of democratic capitalism. Novak uses the example of Niebuhr's conversion to democratic capitalism to illustrate some of the key ideas which affected it.

In the concluding chapter, "Theology of Democratic Capitalism," Dr. Novak tells us that his aim is "to cite Christian doctrines which have been powerful in leading humanity fitfully and slowly to formulate institutional practices and methods which have made economic development, political liberty and a moral cultural commitment to progress on earth, emerge in history as a realistic force."

According to the author, "The ideals a system is designed to serve . . . stimulate each new generation to advance the work of its forebearers. Building a human social order is not a task of one generation merely. It is a journey of a thousand years. For democratic capitalism, only two hundred years have been traversed." This remark is an admission of the imperfection of the system, and it awakens in the heart of a Muslim an appreciation of the merits of his faith, which for fourteen centuries has guided, oriented, and given its adherents strength in face of the vicissitudes of history. Had its progressive spirit not been checked so powerfully by adverse circumstances, it would have kept pace with democratic capitalism, which has in fact built on the foundations of the past achievements of Islam.

In this chapter, Dr. Novak tries to lay the foundation of a new discipline, the theology of economics. It is one of the most fundamental and original sections of the work, though we Muslims may not be able to see eye to eye with Dr. Novak's views here. Some of his remarks touch sensitive nerves and disturb our Muslim conscience since they conflict very sharply with our monotheistic beliefs.

Let us first summarize his views. He hypothesizes that the Christian doctrine of the Trinity may have inspired the notion of "three systems in one" and that the doctrine of the incarnation may have been responsible for the spirit of practicality, humility, concrete thinking, realism, and modest expectations. Discussing the third doctrine, "competition," the author mentions some Christian traditions that regard worldly success as a common obstacle to grace and then concludes by imagining that the virtues which arose from the worldly asceticism of the plain Christian life turned out, under some specific conditions in the urban markets of eighteenth-century Britain and North America, to result in hard work, thrift, savings, prudent investments, and worldly success. He also remarks that political economy needs bold political leaders who thrive in contests of power and willful dreams, and builders who delight in overcoming economic difficulties in order to produce.

The author asserts, on the one hand, that the doctrine of human sinfulness reinforces the realistic spirit of democratic capitalism and leaves no room for dreamy Utopian expectations of a perfect society. On the other hand, this doctrine regards tyranny as the worst type of sin.

As for the fifth Christian doctrine—namely, the separation of church and state—Dr. Novak apparently feels that this doctrine may have inspired the concept of a tripartite political economic system and hence the separation of functions and the mutual respect of the three component systems that make up democratic capitalism. Therefore, in a democratic capitalist society, according to Dr. Novak, moral-cultural institutions may not impose their morality on the other two systems.

The sixth and final doctrine of Christianity, according to Dr. Novak, is love or *caritas*. He describes it as the highest of all theological symbols, the one closest to God's compassion and sacrificial love. He says that its distinguishing feature is that it is realistic love, and he quotes Thomas Aquinas: "To love is to will the good of the other." Building on this, Dr. Novak suggests that love must not be possessive, reducing the loved one to an adjunct to oneself. "Love," he concludes, "is a great teacher of realism about ourselves."

Thus, in the last part of his book, Dr. Novak has tried to defend democratic capitalism from the hostility of Catholics and has demonstrated its superiority over the liberation theology of Latin America and the Christian socialism of Europe. He has also exonerated it from guilt for the third world's poverty. He has analyzed the Christian theological doctrines which he believes must have planted, and for over eighteen hundred years incubated, the seed of the spirit of democratic capitalism, which flowered at a time when the psychological and cultural milieu was ready to receive it.

In the course of his treatment of the concept of development, Dr. Novak relates it to the annual gross national product (GNP) which was given a boost by the mechanism of the patent law, which enhanced the inventive spirit. He says rightly that whereas the GNP can be increased by diligence, steadfast regularity, and responsibly seizing opportunity—thus leading to the diffusion of wealth and prosperity—progress can be hindered by concentrating wealth and power in the hands of a few, by unhealthy control of economic activities, and by unfavorable habits and retarding beliefs and taboos, which are unreasonable avoidances.

Dr. Novak seems to count among factors retarding development abstention from the practice of usury. In his opinion, the concept of usury ought to be modified in view of what he describes as a "modern discovery"—namely, that wealth can create wealth. I am afraid that most Muslim scholars will disagree. They believe that usurious dealings, including paying a fixed rate of interest on bank deposits, are responsible for almost all the evils of our time! It should also be noted that the notion that capital has the power to grow has always existed. It is not merely a modern notion. It was always a stimulus to saving and investment. A simple farmer, for instance, who with his dependents could live on the harvest from one acre, cultivated more acres to grow cash crops to live better and save for himself and his family.

I admire Dr. Novak's remarks in his analysis of the views of the liberation theologians. According to the author, instead of learning from the Bible and then applying their insights to the world, they learn from the world and seek to locate their experiences in the Bible. One wonders whether Dr. Novak himself was pursuing a similar course in first presenting his political economic philosophy and then trying to adduce a theological basis for it from the complex notion of the so-called Judeo-Christian tradition.

Dr. Novak has written at length about conditions in Latin America, and sought to convince his readers that the U.S. political economy cannot be held fully responsible for Latin America's relative economic retardation.

I also admire Dr. Novak's idea of dividing countries into two categories: those naturally endowed and those culturally endowed. Stagnation in those endowed only by nature, such as in South America, occurs as a result of economic control by powerful personages, chauvinism, corruption, and less productive attitudes such as those inspired by the liberation theologians. Those culturally endowed, however, even when they may be less well endowed by nature, like Hong Kong, Singapore, Taiwan, and South Korea, have been able to achieve national prosperity. In such a milieu, factors retarding development are less significant, and cultural values spur hard work and sustained enterprise.

Isn't it true, however, that the superpowers have been contributing a share to this lack of progress? Have they not meddled, sometimes openly, in the affairs of these nations, under the pretext of acting in their own best interests, causing political instability, economic disruption, and retarded development?

Here again, how do we define the national best interests of one country vis-à-vis the national best interests of another country? In my opinion, just as we defined the best interests of an individual as those that do not encroach upon the interests of another person, we must, in the case of international relations, insist that the legitimate best interests of one country do not harm those of another country. In the interest of global peace and prosperity, countries on our small planet, especially those of superior power and greater wealth, should adjust and coordinate their interests with those of the other nations. We cannot, in the context of international relations, apply Adam Smith's thesis and say that when a country works for its own best interests alone, disregarding the fundamental interests of other nations, the sum total of global achievements will lead through the intervention of an invisible hand, to an increase in the total wealth of all nations. There is a difference between the psychology of the individual, who is naturally concerned with his own survival and that of his dependents, and the psychology of government officials, who could be more rational in working on behalf of their country. If government officials do something to hurt other countries, they will in turn hurt their own country. It would be better if moral justice, not expediency, became the primary factor in interactions between people at all levels—on the individual, national, and international levels—because all humanity is one family of families.

Although one admires the stirring and original views enunciated in the concluding chapter of his work, Dr. Novak's theological formulation with due respect to him, though ingenious, is no more than hypothetical guesses. After all, Christianity existed nearly eighteen hundred years before capitalism emerged as an economic school of thought. If Dr. Novak's hypotheses that Christian doctrines slowly and sporadically led humanity toward the spirit of democratic capitalism as a vital force were true, why did it take so many centuries to emerge? And why only in Western society?

One is reluctant to get involved in a religious debate, but how can we conceive of God or speak of Him as our author does, in human terms, while God's existence is inherent and eternal, and He is to be described only by the most perfect attributes? How can we think of God as a community or a loner? How can we apply human psychological terms to our Creator Who is perfectly different? After all, the Trinity is not a universal Christian doctrine. Also, one may wonder why the doctrine of the Trinity could work out with some of its adherents and not with the others! And if we concede its effect

54

among its believers or some of them, how can we still extend this notion and call it a *Judeo*-Christian tradition? Judaism does not espouse a Trinity doctrine. Moreover, the doctrine of Incarnation is inherently contradictory; and the clause of speaking of God in this context by the author—namely, "stooping lowly"—is something abhorrent to the Muslim ear.

The principle of competition is by no means unique to Christian doctrine. The doctrines of sin and the separation of church and state, I believe, are common to all Christian denominations, some of which are very much opposed to democratic capitalism. The doctrine of love mentioned by Dr. Novak can be better claimed by the socialists than by the advocates of capitalism as an inspiration to their own beliefs.

One statement made by the author that Muslims unfortunately cannot endorse is: "In the economic sphere, creation is to be fulfilled through human imitation of the Creator." How can mortals imitate their Creator, unto whom "nothing whatever is like" [Qur'ān 42:11]? We only seek to fulfill God's will through obedience to His commands and through hard work. Nor do we endorse the belief that success in this world is often entirely the opposite of success in the life of grace, which the author seems to support. Does this mean that Americans who are successful democratic capitalists are outside divine grace? As Muslims, we believe that worldly success can be a great blessing. A person who is thus successful can worship God with a more relaxed mind and with a deeper sense of gratitude. He can gain greater merit with God by helping the poor and the needy, and by giving to charitable causes. A successful person works harder and contributes more to the total GNP. He earns a living through legitimate means and pays the required dues to the poor; otherwise, he is not really successful no matter how wealthy he may appear to be.

Lastly, Dr. Novak states that "God regards not the worldly success of man but his response to God's word in his heart and deeds." It is as if Dr. Novak took it from the mouth of the Prophet who said: "God does not look at your form or your wealth, but at your hearts and deeds."[9] Dr. Novak concedes in a concluding statement that democratic capitalism has been harsher than the way he has described it. He is not concerned, he says, with empirical assessment, but he praises the system because of its colossal achievements in economic production, a success badly needed today in view of the frightening rate of increase in the world population.

Notes

1. Michael Novak, *The Spirit of Democratic Capitalism* (New York: An American Enterprise Institute/Simon & Schuster Publication, 1982).

2. According to the Holy Qur'ān: "Say [unto them, Muhammad]: Are those who know equal with those who know not? But only people of understanding will pay heed [39:9]."

3. Ahmad Ibn Hanbal, *Al-Musnad* (Cairo, 1933), vol. 5, p. 145. Cited hereafter as *Al-Musnad*.

4. *Al-Ihya'*, vol. 2, p. 6; *Al-Musnad*, vol. 3, p. 299.

5. Tirmidhi, *Sunan*, vol. 4, p. 35.

6. Ibid., p. 225.

7. This is a wise saying, not a *hadīth*. Cf. Isma'il al-'Ajluni, *Kashf al-Khafa wa Muzil al Iltibas* (Cairo, n.d.), vol. 2, p. 342.

8. Chapter 16, verse 71.

9. Muslim, *Sahih*, vol. 16, p. 121.

3
Islam and Democratic Capitalism: Similarities and Differences

Dr. Michael Novak has envisioned the existence of an intellectual jewel, a philosophy, a moral virtue, a theological basis behind the American political economic system, the pattern of capitalism that the United States inherited from Great Britain but altered and modified "in a social context and a general mood entirely different from those of the nineteenth century." It is as though Dr. Novak felt that this intellectual jewel—which dazzled but eluded Jacques Maritain, the author of the UN Declaration of Universal Human Rights, and Reinhold Niebuhr, whose economic-philosophical thought is traced by the author—was floating aimlessly in the air, and that his task was to grasp this jewel, analyze it, and elucidate it, and then offer it as a theory worthy of actual practice to reformers who may lead the system to a perfect fulfillment of its own dreams of liberty, equality, and justice.

Part of Dr. Novak's task has been to exonerate capitalism from the stigma it has earned since capitalism developed in a climate saturated and polluted by the philosophies of radical individualism, utilitarianism, and social Darwinism, and to expose its merits and virtues. In the course of his reflections, Dr. Novak had to cover a wide range of interesting and relevant topics. He made numerous stirring remarks and thought-provoking observations.

Readers of Dr. Novak's work and of this monograph should be able to appreciate the similarity between some of Dr. Novak's remarks and the ideas found in some of the fourteen centuries old texts I have quoted here from Islamic religious sources. The author's emphasis, for example, on sustained increased production to meet the needs of the rapidly growing global population reminds one of the abundant rewards promised to a believer from the fruits of a tree he has planted, a bird, an animal, or a person he has fed.[1] In order for sustained economic development to be possible, according to Dr. Novak, individuals must believe that they can alter their future. This reminds one of the Qur'ānic statement: "God does not change the condition of a people until they [first] change what is in their hearts."[2] Not only is it important to produce wealth, but how it is used is also important, Dr. Novak continues. This reminds us of the Prophet's warning that each person will be asked by God about his wealth—how he earned it and how he spent it.[3]

The most important and original contribution Dr. Novak makes in his remarkable work is his brilliant analysis of democratic capitalism as three separate, mutually autonomous, but interdependent systems, and his ingenious thesis as to what constitutes, in his view, the theological basis of this political-economic philosophy. The author's analysis of the spirit of democratic capitalism is useful, practical, and appealing. The human individual is indeed a package consisting of spiritual, moral, political, economic, and fickle aspects. Underlying all these aspects is the one fundamental human value: personal self-concern. The direction in which the individual exercises his will power is merely where he perceives his momentary self-interest to be.

The author's analysis of a political system, an economic system, and a moral-cultural system, each having its own institutions, procedures, rituals, and social strengths, fits this reality. Dr. Novak asserts that in order for the spirit of democratic capitalism to work, each of the three components must respect the autonomy of the others, yet each should keep watch over the other's work from a distance, ready to extend a helpful hand when needed. The beneficial results of their independent activities converge and serve the best interests of the nation, indeed of all nations. Each system provides the services it deems necessary to protect or enhance the work of the others. The political system, for example, takes special measures to maintain the soundness of the national currency and promote the country's international trade, which is in the service of the economic system. The state also raises taxes to pay for various services. It imposes minimum wages and introduces regulations to protect the interests of consumers.[4]

The main feature of democratic capitalism, according to Dr. Novak, is the liberty granted to individuals and the respect of their autonomy, thus unleashing the potential of the individual, allowing each person to choose, work, invent, explore, develop, and produce to his fullest capacity unchecked and unhindered. One product of this is the business corporation, which is able to undertake large-scale projects and in which individuals can pool their financial and human resources to maximize profits.

How does Islam differ from democratic capitalism as presented and analyzed by Dr. Novak? Does Islam insist on the separation of the moral-cultural system both from the political system and the economic system? To what extent can the economic system be independent of the political system?

Dr. Novak writes and thinks from a Western background in which religion is highly organized and possesses tremendous power and authority. He is right, I believe, in his effort to protect the economic and political systems from the whims of a priest or clergyman, especially when we bear in mind that Western society views religion as having a degree of dynamism. Doctrines and dogmas may assume different shapes at different times and can be modified by a pope or an influential religious leader or a religious council. In Islam, there is no class of religious men or religious women. There can be no modification of any basic religious truth or a moral principle, since they are believed to have been decreed and prescribed by God Himself, as revealed in history to his Prophets.

Therefore, divine revelation is the point of departure between Islamic beliefs and Dr. Novak's views. Muslims study the text of our Holy Book; we digest it, assisted and augmented by the study of Al-Hadīth. We then apply the insight so gained to the business of our life. In other words, we do not learn from the world and then try to locate our experience in our Holy Book. And thus Islam permeates both the political system and the economic system. We do not separate religion from either politics or economics. Both find inspiration and guidance in our moral-religious system. But religion here means the set of beliefs and dogmas, the total teachings of a faith, independent of an organized class of people or a church.[5]

When we come to the question of separating economics from the political system in a democratic capitalist society, some lack of precision seems to exist in Dr. Novak's analysis. To what extent can a democratic capitalist government step into the realm of economics? Dr. Novak mentions a few areas: government actions to protect the soundness of the national currency, to regulate competition and protect international trade, and to limit negative results of trade and industries, such as pollution. He focuses, however, on economic liberty and a minimum of government intervention.

What distinguishes the American democratic capitalist economy is that, generally speaking, it is privately owned. It is a free enterprise system, an open market economy. Otherwise, it is a shared burden between the citizens and their government. The U.S. Constitution specifies the powers of the federal government: to regulate commerce with other nations, to establish uniform bankruptcy laws, to print money and regulate its value, to fix standards of weights and measures, to establish post offices and post roads, and to establish the rules governing patents and copyrights.[6] The government must also intervene, in the interest of its citizens, in three cases. First, the government can step in if an economic activity will have an adverse effect on the nation or a large segment of the population—hence zoning laws, antipollution laws, laws against dealing in poisonous drugs, and the establishment of consumer agencies. Second, the government may, and must, raise funds in the form of taxation to provide national services, including defense, internal security, and the various welfare services. Third, the government may provide measures that will stimulate greater production or reduce unemployment.

All these, as we can see, do not interfere with the liberty of economic activity or free enterprise. Citizens can choose their way of living as free producers, free consumers, and free voters. A citizen may determine the type of economic activity he wishes to pursue—alone, together with someone else, or in a corporation. As long as he pays his taxes, he may save, invest, and amass any amount of wealth. He may engage in importing and exporting as long as he respects the laws of the government protecting international trade.

Islam is amenable to all these features of the democratic capitalist economy. A Muslim can easily and successfully survive and prosper under democratic capitalism with very little need for adjustment. How, then, does Islam differ economically from democratic capitalism? We have already referred to the fundamental differences regarding the source of the economic thought. Whereas democratic capitalism is a development of human experience, the basis of the economic doctrine of Islam is divinely inspired. Therefore, the economic life of a Muslim is not entirely a materialistic or this-worldly vocation. Its stimulus is derived both from the individual's drive to gain wealth and from his wish to be an obedient servant of God. Thus, intent counts, and the type of economic activity a Muslim engages in must be legitimate. Unlike some democratic capitalists, he cannot take as his profession gambling, cruel sports such as cockfighting or wrestling, trading in harmful drugs such as liquor, or in prostitution, or in pornography. He would even abstain from consuming any food or drink purchased by means of profits gained from such illegal pursuits. Therefore, although democratic capitalism shares with Islam the prohibition of corrupt practices, it differs subtly from Islam in this way: A Muslim who can hide illegal earnings knows full well that he cannot escape the eyes of God and the law and cannot in conscience consume that gain. Many a democratic capitalist, however, may do so without searching his conscience.

Aside from these few but important differences, Islam also differs from democratic capitalism in several specific respects. One is the complex law of the zakat which is a distinctive feature of the Islamic system of economics and consists of payment of a fixed rate due in certain categories of wealth, in addition to a special obligatory charity to be paid at the end of Ramadan, the month of fasting. Thus Islam prescribes annual payments at fixed rates or in a fixed measure. The Ramadan payment, for example, is universal among Muslims, and is to be given away even on behalf of an infant. Moreover, the minimum amount of wealth, from which 2½ percent is to be taken in the zakat is rather low. So the basis of the zakat is wider than the tax base in the democratic capitalist countries, and its rate is fixed. In a democratic capitalist system, the taxable minimum is higher, the rates rise according to income bracket, and they can vary from year to year.

In addition to this difference between the Islamic and the capitalist systems, under the Shari'a law of Islam a man is responsible for the maintenance of his wife even if she has another source of income. He is also responsible for providing a living for his dependent children, needy parents and grandparents, and needy siblings. He must also help needy members of his kin.

Another feature of the Islamic system is the strict prohibition against usury, which is regarded as a grave sin. No matter how society may change, there can be no change in this rule, which has been established by the Holy Book. Whatever God has decreed cannot be modified by mortals.

Otherwise, Islam and democratic capitalism have much in common. Like democratic capitalism, Islam favors open, free markets, free enterprise, and an economy that is privately owned, though a Muslim believes that his ownership of wealth is not absolute.

Quite significantly, both Islam and democratic capitalism view state control of the economy disapprovingly. They regard it as the state's responsibility to: (1) take adequate measures to protect the nation or a segment of the population from actions that might have adverse effects; (2) provide necessary services for which the government may raise taxes to pay their costs; and (3) take measures that will stimulate greater production and greater success of the economy. Otherwise, citizens are free to choose and pursue the economic course each deems to be the best for him. Each is allowed to amass as much wealth as he can, provided it is earned legitimately and that duties are paid.

Dr. Novak's analysis attempts to reduce the role of religion in economics. He refuses to subordinate economic activities to the moral dictates of religion—hence, his hesitation to "Christianize" democratic capitalism. What Dr. Novak tries to do in his book, it seems to me, is to trace those elements in the Judeo-Christian tradition which, he supposes, must have instilled in the minds of the Judeo-Christian nations notions, ideas, and values leading fitfully and slowly over the centuries to the emergence of a powerful force, the spirit behind democratic capitalism. The role of religion, according to Dr. Novak, was remote, slow, and indirect. Like the liberal theologians, the author seems to be learning from the world and then seeking to locate his experience in the Bible.

Our own course has been the reverse, as the reader must have seen. We Muslims study our religious sources, the Holy Qur'ān and *Al-Hadīth*. We digest them, and then try to apply the insight we have thus gained to our lives.

For Muslims, there are only two systems, the political and the economic, since a separate religious class or an organized church is not an Islamic concept. The mosque, the legal property of God without the limits of a parish, has never wielded the power that the Church did in the Middle Ages and to some extent is still doing today. It has been a place of worship and learning; and though it has sometimes been a place for political meetings it is not a center of political power. Religious scholars, the Muslim theologians, may give their viewpoints and provide guidance, but they may not give technical advice on how to run the economy. In this respect, we are in sympathy with Dr. Novak. The Prophet said: "You know better the affairs of your earthly life."[7]

Islam, which is well known for its practicality and sensible spirit, and which makes justice and the recognition and respect of fundamental human rights cardinal duties, agrees with much of Dr. Novak's criticism of socialism. It disapproves of the harsh measures of the socialists and the oppressive control of the economy by the state, though a degree of intervention by the state in the best interests of the nation is tolerable to the degree explained earlier. Moreover, Islam welcomes diversity in unity or, rather, unity in diversity. Citizens of various religions and ideological beliefs may engage together in trade or industry, just as human beings. Islam does not favor harmful central control or creating a center with peripheries. We therefore endorse Dr. Novak's thesis of communalism and pluralism, as is evidenced in the rise of urban Muslim centers simultaneously as a result of intense economic activity. In past centuries, during the glorious age of Islam, splendid and prosperous parallel urban centers flourished all over the vast Muslim empire—Cairo, San'a, Tunis, Fez, Cordova, Baghdad, Bukhara, Samarkand, Damascus, Timbuktu, and Katsina, to name only a few. Traders and merchants as well as scholars, as history indicates, traveled widely and easily between these great centers of commerce and learning. They conducted business and increased their knowledge, assisted by the local guilds of their respective trades in these centers.

On visiting Islamic exhibits in major museums in the West or Islamic museums in the capitals of Islamic countries, one gains a sense of the high level of achievement, of the great skill, dexterity, and knowledge of these early industrious Muslims. There are also the magnificent Islamic monuments in Spain and North Africa and in Middle Eastern and Asian cities.

As in democratic capitalism, time in Islam is regarded as a valuable commodity to be invested profitably and not to be wasted. It is incumbent on every adult believer, for example, to pray within a prescribed period of time, five times each day. A regard for the value of time is also inspired by associating other ritual duties with some special days of the year and by recalling such traditions as the following:

> The feet of the son of Adam will not cross the Bridge (over the Hellfire leading to Paradise on the other side) unless he answers satisfactorily as to how he had used his lifetime, how he dispensed of his youthful energy, how he earned his wealth, and how he spent it.[8]

Islam rejects the doctrine of original sin and teaches that every person is born innocent and free of any traces of guilt or bondage. It denies that man is in need of redemption or baptism, though it recognizes man's susceptibility to making errors. He is therefore called upon to resist the temptation of sin, which simply means disobedience to the teaching of God. Resisting evil temptation is a virtue to be rewarded by God. Among those violations counted as sins are gambling, usury, and trading in liquor or other harmful materials.

Because of its emphasis on equality, some may naively regard the economic system of Islam as a form of socialism.[9] This is not so. Equality, in the sense of socialism, means equality in wealth, in income. Islam, however, teaches equality of opportunity, not of fortune. How can Islam be likened to an oppressive system that denies the individual his liberty and his right to possess property? Still, some others may think that Islam, because it defends liberty and endorses personal ownership, is one variety of capitalism.[10] This is not so either. To repeat, ownership in Islam is not absolute as it is in capitalism. In Islam it is a concept of double ownership, as God is the real and ultimate owner of all that is in heaven and on earth. Another significant divergence of Islam from capitalism is Islam's interest in the person's motive and its insistence on the legitimacy of his economic action, not only in the ultimate outcome as is the case with capitalism. Both socialism and capitalism are human philosophies, but the economic doctrine of Islam has its roots in divine revelation. Whereas the man-made systems of socialism and capitalism are simply materialistic, the Islamic system pays great attention to man's spiritual nature.

Even when we concede any degree of affinity between Islam and either of the two modern philosophies of political economics, we hesitate to call the Islamic system of economics either capitalism or socialism or, for that matter, a democratic capitalist or a democratic socialist economy. The economic system of Islam is just a part of the whole Islamic guidance, and therefore has to coordinate and cooperate with other parts of this totality. Similarly, the political system of Islam has no special title. We hesitate to call it a democracy, theocracy, oligarchy, or even a republic or a kingdom. All is simply Islam or Islamic.

As we have seen in the treatment of Islamic economies, each segment of the total Islamic doctrine is based on relevant texts in the Holy Qur'ān and *Al-Hadīth*. These texts either consist of specific terms or are couched in general terms. When teachings appear in specific terms, they are to be taken as given. This gives the system its Islamic character. When teachings are couched in general terms, Muslims are at liberty to interpret them, within the limits of the term, as may suit the needs of time and context. This dynamism gives the Islamic moral guidance a degree of flexibility and adaptability and has made Muslims, for the past fourteen centuries, able to adapt to all conditions and environments. They have never changed the basic tenets of Islam and have never sought to reinterpret the prohibition against eating pork, consuming liquor, or practicing usury. They have never modified the prescribed manner of worship or changed their attitude toward avoiding all forms of premarital and extramarital relations and modern forms of living together outside the bond of marriage. Otherwise, the system would lose its Islamic character.

The need of the Europeans to adopt labels to denote their modern political or economic thought probably arose from the need to break with their oppressive past in an identifiable way. Under the feudal system during the Middle Ages, as Dr. Novak explains, the social status of the individual, his vocation, and his religion were determined at birth once and for all. The nobility and its allies formed the center, and the rest of the population was the oppressed periphery. The individual was subsumed within his community. As a reaction to this oppressive time, when trade and industry were despised and progress was held back, the Renaissance in Europe emphasized

64

the concept of individualism in a radical way. Capitalism, it seems, caught on to this theme, and socialism reacted against it. Democratic capitalism, in Dr. Novak's terms, sought to strike a balance, harmonizing individual liberty with communal obligations within a pluralistic frame work.

Readers of these views may be surprised when they look around them and see that many of the powers in command of more than forty Muslim countries arrogantly pose as socialist regimes. The world of Islam is currently in a stage of transition and confusion and has suffered oppression at the hand of deceived (Muslim) politicians. To them the term "socialism" is an empty but good-sounding word, which they apply to any form of government that suits them, to deceive their citizens and intimidate their adversaries. They are interested in the dictatorial method of socialism, whereby they seek to perpetuate their own rule, leaving no effective voice for opposition. Hence, there is a current wave of resurgence among Muslims who wish to correct the situation and see the true Islamic way of government restored, so that each citizen can enjoy the fresh air of freedom. Those oppressive (Muslim) rulers are violating the tenets of their own faith, which, probably more than any other religion, struggled, and indeed succeeded, in restoring fundamental human rights of each person. So the economic liberty of a Muslim springs from his own religion.

Dr. Novak's romantic attempt to link the spirit of democratic capitalism to six Christian doctrines—the Trinity, the Incarnation, confession, original sin, the separation of realms, and love—is not only too complicated, but, in my judgment, is a product of imagination and guesswork. One may wonder why these doctrines did not work in the same way with Eastern Christianity.

If we may venture to offer a theory as to the roots of the emergence in Western society of institutionalized political liberty, economic liberty, and a commitment to progress, the three ingredients of democratic capitalism, it seems that these roots can be traced to the fertile intellectual ferment in Western Europe in the wake of the disintegration of the feudal system, when the individual's right to liberty was stressed, awakening in him an inner feeling of his creative ability. Other contributing factors, it seems, were the rise of urban clusters, with new values honoring work, trade, and industry, and the spirit of adventurousness released through colonization and the discovery of hitherto unknown lands, people, and vast economic resources. The deep rupture with the past and with its oppression, man's newly awakened confidence in his own inventive powers, and the availability of huge sources of raw materials fired the imagination of the people and led to the invention of machinery which made it possible to build large-scale industries. All this, coupled with the Protestant spirit, like that of Islam, nourished man's worldly vocation and led to the emergence of capitalism in Western society.

The Founding Fathers of the United States, already filled with the capitalist spirit and realizing the necessity of hard work for survival, intensified and refined capitalism, breathing into it a new spirit, creating new kinds of institutions, and developing healthier structures in the capitalistic mold.

However harsh our criticism of Dr. Novak's thesis for a theological basis of democratic capitalism, one finds his views less rhetorical and more profound and scholarly than George Gilder's argument for a "theology of capitalism" and his philosophy of the supply side, as enunciated in his article "The Moral Sources of Capitalism"[11] and as further elucidated in his book *Wealth and Poverty*. Gilder's criticism of Adam Smith's theory of self-interest is uncharitable and unjustified. Looking after one's self-interest is not the same as greed or personal avarice. Gilder's claim that capitalism "calls forth, propagates, and relies upon the best and most generous of human qualities,"[12] is an obvious exaggeration. So is his arbitrary assertion that "Altruism is the essence of capitalism!"[13] Was it altruistic of the capitalist colonial masters to cut off the fingers of workers in factories in colonized territories to eliminate competition with their goods? Can the attitude today of the lords of capitalism toward the poor third-world nations be called altruistic? Dr. Novak's treatment is more sensible and closer to reality.

Neither capitalism nor socialism can be an alternative to Islam. A confused equality is the aim of socialism; and unfettered liberty is the ideal of capitalism. Socialism focuses on distribution; and capitalism focuses on more production. Socialists have sought but failed to establish, through state control, a new social order without classes, racial barriers, poverty, or personal property. Through laissez faire, capitalists have succeeded in establishing an order of liberty and sustained growth. The result has been great leaps forward in technological progress, which has considerably transformed the pattern of human life but has also caused alienation and domestic fragmentation.

The objective of Islam for man on earth is freedom from want and success in serving his Lord. The focus of Islam is on peace and the well-being of both the individual and the society. It guarantees the individual's right to dignity and liberty, to the equal opportunity to work, learn, earn, own, and move about as he chooses within the limits of justice to his fellow men. The Islamic ideal is to pursue a

progressive but contented life which partakes of life's legitimate pleasures and the bounties in a moderate way. The spiritual and the
worldly needs are fulfilled, and the individual's concerns and those of
the community are reconciled, coordinated, and harmonized.

Dr. Novak's attempt to develop a moral-cultural basis or, rather,
a theological basis for "democratic" capitalism is an effort to remedy
the materialistic stigma of capitalism and to dress it with some moral
value. That attempt has not been a complete success, one should say,
but not a complete failure either. His wisdom in insisting on the
separation and mutual independence of the economic system and the
political system, in the sense we advocated previously, is supported
by the failure of socialist regimes to reconcile the ideology of state
control with the best interests of the national economy.

Aside from the current tension existing between the so-called
North and South, or between the developed and the developing nations, the best lesson people in the third-world countries can learn
from Dr. Novak's remarkable work, and from the Western experience
in general, is the value and wisdom of recognizing and respecting the
autonomy of the economic sphere, the merits of an equitable distribution of power, the advantages of honoring individual liberty, and the
virtues of careful planning, hard work, and devotion to duty—all of
which are basic parts of the noble teachings of Islam. So let those in
power trust to the integrity and loyalty of their citizens and reduce
their interference in the economic realm. Let them reflect on the fact
that although technological progress is so slow at home, their own
countrymen who have settled in democratic societies, where they
have flourished, have been able to compete successfully with their
European and American counterparts and to make valuable contribu-
tions in all technological and scientific fields as well as in commerce
and industry. Why can't they do the same at home, in the countries of
their birth?

May I at this juncture respectfully address myself to our friends
in the West. We earnestly urge them to go back to God, to turn their
face toward Him. While continuing the struggle for material progress,
they must remember God's bounties. They should abandon harmful
business that is contrary to the capitalist ideal of sustained productivity. Members of the family should stay closer together and be more
faithful and loyal to one another. What was morally right for Noah,
Abraham, Moses, Jesus, and Muhammad must be the same for us—
whether we live in America, Europe, Asia, or Africa.

We all should remember that we are brothers, members of the
large human family. Let us live together in peace, in love and sincere
cooperation, each giving freely and ungrudgingly from what he has.

Let the spirit of democratic capitalism, the ultimate aim of socialism, and the Islamic aspiration of universal brotherhood dominate and collaborate for peace and prosperity on earth.

In conclusion, I trust that my readers will agree that there are many good things in common between Islam and the Christian democratic capitalist world. Apart from the fact that we Muslims believe in the Christian Gospel, the Christian Prophet, his twelve Apostles, his mother's purity, and his miraculous birth, we also share a belief in the individual's worth and liberty, in the protection of his property, and equality. Above all, we share a belief in our Lord, our common God Who has provided abundance and made it ready for all to use, enjoy, and develop in a way befitting human dignity. These significant common features not only make it possible for a Muslim living in a democratic capitalist society to flourish and thrive, but can also serve as a bridge of understanding, cooperation, and collaboration between the world of Islam and the West.

Notes

1. Ahmad Ibn Hanbal, *Al-Musnad* (Cairo, 1933), vol. 4, p. 132.
2. Qur'ān, chap. 13, verse 11.
3. Muslim Ibn al-Hajjaj, *Sahih* (with commentary by Imam al-Nawawi) (Beirut, 1978), vol. 10, pp. 213–15; Ahmad Ibn Hanbal, *Al-Musnad* (Cairo, 1933), vol. 3, p. 140. Cf. Tirmidhi, *Sunan*, vol. 7, p. 101.
4. In a Muslim situation, the Muslim government must force reluctant citizens to pay alms to the poor, recalcitrant craftsmen to manufacture needed articles on receiving fair payment for them, and greedy traders hoarding food stuffs to sell their goods at fair prices to feed hungry citizens. According to early jurists, a Muslim government must also protect the Muslim market, to ensure that it runs smoothly and uses accurate weights and measures; it must regulate trade with foreign nations and impose customs duties on imported goods equal to those imposed by foreign authorities on Muslim exports.
5. A distinction must be made between religion, culture, and morality. The first term covers all teachings supposed to be revealed by God. A culture of a people is comprehensive and includes their religious beliefs and practices, their language and all the habits and customs they may have developed throughout history. A culture includes religious and human elements. Moral behavior to Muslims has to be inspired, endorsed, and guided by religious revelation. The moral conscience must be nourished and supported by the religious guidance—thus, moral postulates are perpetual and cannot be left to personal whims. We have seen a lowering of morality, openly justified on the pretext that an act only involves mutually consenting adults. "There can be no two persons alone except that God is the third" (Qur'ān 58:7). God's consent is more important to make an act agreeable.

68

6. Robert McCan, *An Outline of the American Economics* (International Communication Agency, U.S. Department of State, n.d.) p. 3. See also pp. 12 and 71ff.

7. Muslim, *Sahih*, vol. 15, pp. 116–18. In this context, the Prophet adds: "I am [only] a human being. If I convey to you something on behalf of God accept it as given. But if I should offer an opinion regarding a worldly matter, your experience may be a greater wisdom."

8. Muslim, *Sahih*, vol. 10, pp. 213–15.

9. See, for example, Muhammad Akbar Muradpur, *Conflict between Socialism and Islam* (Lahore, 1970), p. 1, and an Egyptian publication by the Ministry of National Guidance, *Muslimun Ishtirakiyyun* [Muslim socialists], 1960s.

10. Maxime Rodinson, *Islam and Capitalism*, trans. (New York: Pantheon Books, 1973), pp. 1 f and 118 f.

11. George Gilder, "The Moral Sources of Capitalism," in *Imprimis* (Hillside College, Michigan), vol. 9, no. 12 (December 1980), pp. 1–6.

12. Ibid., p. 2.

13. Ibid., p. 4.

Bibliography

Al-Qur'ān

Al-Qur'ān, or the Koran, the Holy Book believed by Muslims to be the Word of God revealed to the Prophet Muhammad, consists of 114 chapters of varying length. Chapter 2, the longest, comprises 268 verses and chapter 108, the shortest, consists of 3 short verses. The text had to be transmitted orally, but it was also written during the life of the Prophet and was duplicated for distribution shortly after his death. The Qur'ān is significant as the main source of Islamic guidance and also as a text of prayers, the recitation of which is of great merit.

Abdallah Yusuf Ali. *The Holy Qur'ān, Text, Translation and Commentary*, The Islamic Center, Washington, D.C., 1975.

Mohammed Marmaduke Pickthall. *The Meaning of the Glorious Qur'ān*, The New American Library, 1963.

Al-Hadīth

Al-Hadīth, is the record of the Prophet Muhammad's sayings, deeds, and silently approved acts done under his eye. Since the Qur'ān states that the Prophet was a model of behavior for his followers and that whatever he taught should be accepted, *Al-Hadīth* has become the second authority on Islamic guidance. Fears over the integrity of the text of the Holy Qur'ān delayed the writing down of *Al-Hadīth* for nearly ten decades, when these fears dissipated as a result of the text of the Qur'ān becoming universally distinct from any other sayings. Then those who were recognized as authorities on the *hadīth* sciences began to commit to writing what had hitherto been entrusted to memory, taking every precaution against making errors. Therefore, each *hadīth* had to be introduced by the series of teachers who transmitted the *hadīth* from the Prophet down to the writer himself. Each transmitter in this series, which became known as *isnad* ("support"), had to be widely known in his time as a great authority on *hadīth* and must have been a person of piety and integrity, and one who feared God. Anything less than this was rejected. Moreover, each narrator in the *isnad* must be known to have possessed a powerful, vivid memory up to the time of his death. Any weakness that might have occurred would weaken the reliability of the *hadīth* in question.

The list that follows gives the major *hadīth* compilations that are widely recognized and respected all over the world of Islam. Because each author learned from a number of teachers, he could have more than one *isnad* for a single *hadīth*, hence a number of *hadīth* texts can be repeated in a single work, and one *hadīth* text can be found in a number of these books related through different *isnads*. Also, the total number of *hadīths* in each of these compilations may be greater than the number given in my list, as I have omitted the repeated numbers.

Most of the *hadīths* I have quoted in this work are among the popular ones that contributed to the process of building up and sustaining a spectrum of values and ideals which guide Muslims in their struggle for survival. In the notes to the text I have usually quoted only one source and occasionally two. After the first citation, I have used abbreviated forms of these sources.

Abu Dawud, Sulayman Ibn Al-Ash'ath, better known as Abu Dawud, (d.A.H.275/A.D.888). *Sunan* [compilation of prophetic traditions]. Contains 4,800 *hadīths*.

Ahmad Ibn Hanbal (d.241/855). *Al-Musnad* [Traditions traced to the Prophet]. 30,000 *hadīths*.

Bukhari, al-, Muhammad Ibn Isma'il, better known as Al-Bukhari (d.256/870). *Al-Jami' Al-Sahih* [The comprehensive compilation of authentic *hadīths*]. 3,460 *hadīths*. This work as well as that of Muslim are regarded as the most authentic books after the Holy Qur'ān because the authors omitted all *hadīths* in the *isnads* of which there could be some doubt arising from lack of perfect knowledge about the memory or the character of one of the narrators of the *hadīth*. They also added some other prerequisites for the acceptance of any *hadīth* for inclusion in their works.

Ibn Majah, Muhammad Ibn Yazid, better known as Ibn Majah (d.273/886). *Sunan*, 4,341 *hadīths*.

Malik Ibn Anas (d.179/795). *Al-Muwatta'* [smoothed-out work]. 1,720 *hadīths*.

Muslim Ibn Al-Hajjaj, simply known as Muslim (d.261/875). *Sahih* [authentic *hadīths*]. 4,000 *hadīths*.

Nasa'i, al-, Ahmad Ibn Shu'ayb, better known as Al-Nasa'i (d.303/ 915). *Sunan*, 5,000 *hadīths*.

Tirmidhi, al-, Muhammad Ibn 'Isa, better known as Al-Tirmidhi (d.279/892). *Sunan*, 4,000 *hadīths*.

General Works

Abdul-Rauf, Muhammad. *Islam, Faith and Devotion*. Islamic Publications Bureau, Lagos, Nigeria, 1974.

'Ajluni, al-, Isma'il Ibn Muhammad. *Kashf al-Khafa wa Muzil al-Ilbas* [Removing the confusion from and explaining the truth about the popular *hadīths* which are often repeated on the tongues of the people] Beirut, n.d. This is an interesting work whose author flourished in the early part of the eighteenth century. It helps locate popular *hadīths* in the classical works and indicates sayings popularly but mistakenly thought of as *hadīths*.

'Assal, al-, Ahmad, and 'Abd al-Karim Fathi. *Al-Nizam Al-Iqtisadi fi'l-Islam* [The economic system in Islam]. Wahba Press, Cairo, 1977.

'Awad, Badawi 'Abd Allatif. *Al-Nizam Al-Mali fi'l-Islam* [The monetary system in Islam]. The Supreme Council on Islamic Affairs, Cairo, 1972.

Brohi, A. K. *Iqbal and the Concept of Islamic Socialism*. Karachi: Al-Kasimi Press, 1967.

Dusuki, al-, Muhammad. *Al-Malu fi'l-Islam* [Wealth in Islam]. Supreme Council on Islamic Affairs, Cairo, 1978.

Fudayli, al-, 'Abd al-Hadi. *Mushkilat Al-Faqr* [The problem of poverty]. Beirut, 1975.

Galbraith, John Kenneth, and Necole Salinger, *Almost Everyone's Guide to Economics*. New York: Bantam, N.Y., 1980.

Ghazzali, al-, Muhammad, better known as Al-Ghazzali. *Ihya' 'ulum Al-Din* [Revival of the sciences of religion]. Cairo, n.d. The author, Imam Muhammad al-Ghazzali (d.565/1111), is one of the greatest historical personalities in Islam, and this work has had immense influence.

Guillaume, Alfred. *The Life of Muhammad*. London: Oxford University Press, 1955.

Hamza, M. I. *Muslim Socialism and the Western Theories of Socialism*. Supreme Council on Islamic Affairs, Cairo, 1964.

Mahmud, Mustafa. *Al-Markusiyyah wa'l-Islam* [Marxism and Islam]. Ma'arif Press, Cairo, 1975.

Mubarak, al-, Muhammad. *Nizam Al-Islam Al-Iqtisadi* [The Islamic system of economics]. Dar al-Fikr, Beirut, 1978.

Muradpuri, Muhammad Akbar. *Conflict between Socialism and Islam.* Lahore, Pakistan, 1970.

Novak, Michael. "The Right to Development." In Michael Novak and Richard Schifter, *Rethinking Human Rights.* Foundation for Democratic Education, 1981.

———, ed. *Democracy and Mediating Structures: A Theological Inquiry.* American Enterprise Institute, Washington, D.C., 1980.

Qaradawi, al-, Yusuf. *Mushkilat Al-Faqr wa Kayfa 'Alaja-ha 'l-Islam* [The problem of poverty and how Islam has sought to treat it]. Maktabat Al-Aqsa, Amman, Jordan, 1966.

Rodinson, Maxime. *Islam and Capitalism* (trans. from French). New York: Pantheon Press, 1970.

Roman, Stephen, and Eugen Loebl, *The Responsible Society.* Regina Ryan Books, New York, 1977.

Sadr, al-, Muhammad Baqir. *Iqtisaduna* [Our economics]. Ta'aruf Press, Beirut, 1981.

———. *Madha Ta'rifu 'an Al-Iqtisad Al-Islami?* [What do you know about Islamic economics?]. Dar al-Tawhid, Kuwait A.H. 1388.

Siddiqi, Muhammad Nejatullah. *The Economic Enterprise in Islam.* Islamic Publications Ltd., Lahore, 1972.

World Muslim Congress. *Some Economic Aspects of Islam.* Umma Publishing House, Karachi, 1964.

———. *Some Economic Resources of Muslim Countries.* Umma Publishing House, Karachi, 1964.

SELECTED AEI PUBLICATIONS

Humanism and Capitalism:
A Survey of Thought on Morality and the Economic Order

BERNARD MURCHLAND

Examining the anticommercial bias in the writings of classical humanists in England and America, Murchland criticizes contemporary humanists for relying too heavily on premodern canons of criticism.

"Bernard Murchland has made an important contribution to the task of bridging the commercial arts to the liberal arts. This task is of high priority in our universities today." *Professor John Houck, University of Notre Dame*
62 pp./1984/paper 3529-9 $3.95

Toward a Theology of the Corporation

MICHAEL NOVAK

Novak describes the political and moral-cultural systems on which corporations depend for their existence and shows that the corporation has goals and requirements beyond those of the economic system alone. He argues that corporate life is related to high moral-cultural ideals, in the light of which the conduct of corporations may be held to scrupulous account.
56 pp./1981/paper 3432-2 $4.25

The American Vision: An Essay on the Future
of Democratic Capitalism

MICHAEL NOVAK

Novak explores the links within the three-in-one American system—the political, economic, and cultural systems that constitute liberal democratic capitalism. He offers original insights into the experiences of liberty, equality, and fraternity under democratic capitalism and the competition between the business elite and the "new class" and presents a strategy for a spirited intellectual offensive on the part of democratic capitalism.
60 pp./1978/paper 3324-5 $4.25

Democracy and Mediating Structures: A Theological Inquiry

MICHAEL NOVAK, editor

Theologians, professors, and representatives of labor unions and corporations explore the problems of sustaining social institutions in a democratic society. Discussion focuses on mediating structures—the family, church, corporation, and labor unions—that stand between the individual and the larger public institutions.
216 pp./1980/paper 2176-X $7.25/cloth 2175-1 $13.25

Religion and Politics:
The Intentions of the Authors of the First Amendment

MICHAEL J. MALBIN

Malbin argues that the modern Supreme Court's position that Congress must maintain strict neutrality between religion and irreligion has almost reversed the original understanding of the First Amendment. Analyzing the debates in

the First Congress, he shows that the authors meant only to prevent Congress from preferring any particular religious sects over others and from harming existing state religious establishments.
40 pp./1978/paper 3302–4 $3.25

To Empower People:
The Role of Mediating Structures in Public Policy

PETER L. BERGER and RICHARD JOHN NEUHAUS

The authors' classic presentation of their alternative to conservative fears and liberal disillusionment about public policies argues that public policy not only should refrain from weakening or undercutting family, neighborhood, church, voluntary association, and ethnic and racial subcultures but should use them to advance indispensable social goals.
45 pp./1977/paper 3236–2 $3.25

Church, State, and Public Policy

JAY MECHLING, editor

Conferees look for the "new shape" of church-state relations in the light of the abortion controversy, IRS efforts to narrow the definition of tax-exempt religious activities and to regulate church-related schools, and the Labor Department's proposal to bring parochial schools under its supervision of employment practices.
119 pp./1979/paper 2160–3 $5.25/cloth 2159–X $12.25

www.ingramcontent.com/pod-product-compliance
Lightning Source LLC
Jackson TN
JSHW011941131224
75386JS00041B/1504